W9-AHZ-219

Maximizing
LinkedIn
for
Sales and
Social Media
Marketing

ADVANCE PRAISE FOR

Maximizing LinkedIn for Sales and Social Media Marketing

"Neal Schaffer is an important voice in the social business movement today. His deep understanding of how LinkedIn operates as a business tool is invaluable."

—BEVERLY MACY, CEO, Gravity Summit and coauthor of
The Power of Real-Time Social Media Marketing

"The definitive guide for B2B sales & marketing professionals to generate real business on LinkedIn."

—JON FERRARA, founder and CEO of the visionary social CRM platform Nimble

"For the vast majority of sales and business development professionals out there, LinkedIn is a largely untapped resource ripe for the picking. Neal Schaffer props up the ladder and hands you the bucket with this book. Read it, learn it, and start driving business through LinkedIn!"

—JASON FALLS, SocialMediaExplorer.com and coauthor of *No Bullshit Social Media: The All-Business, No Hype Guide to Social Media Marketing*

"Neal Schaffer puts together a step-by-step way for any business of any size to attract and retain customers by leveraging LinkedIn. Leave out the guess work and grab this gem!"

—JOE PULIZZI, Founder, Content Marketing Institute and
coauthor of *Get Content Get Customers*

Neal is a very talented marketer with a deep understanding of LinkedIn and B2B social media. His latest book is a must read as he enlightens the reader with action-able advice on a lucrative platform

—JODEE RICH, CEO, PeopleBrowsr, the social analytics company

"In *Maximizing LinkedIn*, Neal Schaffer delivers the definitive guide to making LinkedIn an integral part of your strategy to build your network, connect with hard-to-reach prospects and grow your business. Buy it. Use it!"

—BOB THOMPSON, founder and CEO, CustomerThink Corp.

"Do you want a crystal-clear book that tactically stitches together the frayed mess between sales, marketing and social media? Do you want a book that explains to your company how to take on he 16th biggest website in the world? If you're a B2B marketer that wants to see serious results, from the social web, put this baby on your desk. And don't take my word for it—just ask Kelly Ducey from the Irish Dog Bloody Mary Company—you can find here on LinkedIn, driving her business."

—ADAM METZ, author of the Amazon.com business best-seller
The Social Customer and *There Is No Secret Sauce*

"If you are a sales or marketing professional in the B2B space, this book is a must read. Mr. Schaffer provides a step-by-step approach for developing new business by engaging with the powerful LinkedIn platform. Maximizing LinkedIn offers many new and creative ways to maximize your time and ultimately your success with LinkedIn."

—ARNIE KUENN, President, Vertical Measures and author of *Accelerate*!

"Neal's new book not only shows how a business of any size can effectively leverage LinkedIn to generate business, but also provides a great collection of practical case studies to bring the book to life. With nearly two decades of successful B2B sales and business development experience under his belt, Neal shares his invaluable knowledge with the world in a useful, applicable way."

—CASSANDRA PEAN, PR Manager, Vocus

"Neal Schaffer goes from soup to nuts in guiding all levels of marketing on how best to use LinkedIn as a meaningful sales and lead generation solution. Practical, actionable, readable: This book is a must-read for anyone wanting to use LinkedIn for competitive advantage."

—PHIL HOLLOWS, CEO and Founder, Feedblitz.com and
author of *List Building for Bloggers*

"Neal delivers unique tips, tricks and techniques along with superior personal insight into what smart actions on LinkedIn can transform our businesses."

—NANCE ROSEN, author of *Speak Up! & Succeed: How to get everything
you want in meetings, presentations and conversations*

"As a professional who has built his personal and professional brand using LinkedIn, I can unequivocally say this: Neal Schaffer gets it! I highly recommend this book to any business—or professional—that wants to truly understand the power of LinkedIn and how to use it to succeed in social media marketing."

—CHUCK HESTER, Chief Connections Officer, Chuck Hester Enterprises

"Neal shows how we can use LinkedIn as a tool to generate sales but also build credibility, brand, and most importantly relationships. A must read book."

—AARON LEE, founder, AskAaronLee.com

"Neal Schaffer is truly one of social media's pioneers, and a leader in teaching how any individual, small business or corporation can apply LinkedIn to their advantage."

—Bob Fine, founder of The Social Media Monthly magazine

"Neal Schaffer took his second LinkedIn book far above and beyond a "how to" but actually provides profound insights in the inner workings of social media in business and how it impacts all of our business lives. I highly recommend it to sales and marketing managers in all sizes of companies. Being one of the first LinkedIn users myself (ID 8573) I can say this book is excellent."

—Axel Schultze, CEO, Xeesm Corp. and Chairman, Social Media Academy

"Unlike many social media "experts" Neal Schaffer is not simply enamored with the technology for its own sake. He balances his knowledge and enthusiasm for social media with a real world grounding in business development. In his new book, Neal cuts through the clutter and gets to what works—to help make LinkedIn work for you and your business."

—Kathy Simmons, President & CEO, Netshare

"So you have been told that you must use LinkedIn to increase your customer base and sales ROI. But how do you get started? I highly recommend Neal Schaffer's new book *Maximizing LinkedIn*. This book will easily guide beginners and experts on how to use LinkedIn to achieve their required results. Read it, share it and use it."

—Michael Carrillo, Co-Founder, CPGjobs (creators of CPGjoblist.com)

"Neal has been a wonderful resource to me and other attorneys on how to use social media effectively. This book will be my reference material of choice when questions or issues come up regarding LinkedIn."

—Michelle Sherman, attorney and consultant to businesses on the legal, regulatory and compliance issues relating to their social media use.

"Neal Schaffer blows me away with his vast knowledge, ability to clearly define effective strategies and how to measure results. He knows his "game" and understands how to navigate the often confusing social media landscape. Trust me, do what Neal says in this book and you'll see results!"

—Joe Rogers, CEO, LOVE Reusable Bags

"Neal has a focused, engaging and uncanny way of delivering insights into how to best leverage what to some might be considered the mystery of LinkedIn. From the perspective of a business-to-business marketing and sales leader, this book helps me cut through the clutter and establish an effective organizational LinkedIn engagement plan that delivers results."

—GREG REWERS, Vice President of Marketing, Louis and Company

"Neal Schaffer certainly has his finger on the pulse of Business 2.0. If you are looking for a compelling read on LinkedIn marketing from a thought leader in the social media space, this is your book!"

—JACK MOLISANI, Executive Director, The LavaCon Conference on Digital Media and Content Strategies

"Neal Schaffer's book contains a wealth of practical, actionable steps to leveraging LinkedIn to generate new business and improve your B2B social media marketing. Professionals in the worlds of sales, business development, and marketing—as well as entrepreneurs and small business owners—will find great value in this informative resource. An internationally recognized speaker on the subject of social media marketing, Neal practices what he preaches and always impresses me with his ability to connect with his audience and provide sound, simple-to-follow advice. Much as he is in person, Neal's book is entertaining, engaging and ever informative. This is a must have for your business reading arsenal."

—THERESA BOYCE, Chair and CEO, CEO Trust

"Neal's book is a practical, easy to read guide for those striving for innovative solutions to develop business on LinkedIn. It helps business professionals power-up their Internet and integrated marketing potential to reach and interact with others to promote their products and services. An invaluable tool for strategic relationship building on the largest professional networking platform in the world with intrinsic and extrinsic value that takes six degrees of separation to a new definition of business success."

—DEBBIE MOYSYCHYN, MBA, Director, Health & Wellness, Brandman University

Maximizing
LinkedIn

for

Sales and
Social Media
Marketing

An Unofficial, Practical Guide to Selling &
Developing B2B Business on LinkedIn

NEAL SCHAFFER

Contents

Preface

IT HAS BEEN APPROXIMATELY 21 MONTHS SINCE I PUBLISHED MY FIRST book about LinkedIn, *Windmill Networking: Understanding, Leveraging & Maximizing LinkedIn.* As a first-time author, I was ecstatic that it received a few prestigious book industry awards, including silver recognition as the best business reference book of the year in 2009 from the Axiom Business Book Awards and honorable mention as the best non-fiction book of 2009 from the DIY Book Festival. And even as I write this new book, I am honored that my first book still remains one of the best-selling LinkedIn books. If you have already bought *Windmill Networking: Understanding, Leveraging & Maximizing LinkedIn* (hereafter referred to as *Windmill Networking: Maximizing LinkedIn*), I want to thank you for your support.

One of the initial book reviews I received after publishing *Windmill Networking: Maximizing LinkedIn,* was a criticism that my book suffered from a "personality complex." In other words, was it a book for businesses or merely about networking? The answer to that question is that my first book was meant to be a reference manual for professionals in every industry to truly maximize LinkedIn for whatever objective they might have. I believe that, at the very least, all professionals should be on LinkedIn to develop and/or better represent their personal brands, even if they are happily employed, networking, and enhancing their brands in other ways. Ideally, however, they should all understand the functionalities of LinkedIn as well as the concept of Windmill Networking, which allows people in all industries to better represent and grow their brands and professional careers.

This book, *Maximizing LinkedIn for Sales and Social Media Marketing,* is meant to be a companion to *Windmill Networking: Maximizing LinkedIn.*

Anybody actively working in the business world knows it is a social venture, so it should come as no surprise that the ability to successfully network has been a necessary skill that sales professionals have honed from the early days of capitalism (if not earlier), yet I find so few people are reaching their full networking potential on the LinkedIn platform. In the capacity of a sales and marketing professional, I have spoken to thousands of people about maximizing LinkedIn for business purposes, and I have consulted with more than a dozen companies of all sizes from a variety of industries on how they can strategically utilize social media, including LinkedIn. In addition, I have successfully executed campaigns related to B2B sales, business development, and marketing over my nearly two decades of working with the business community.

This collection of experiences makes me uniquely qualified to write this book, which is specifically designed to help business owners, executives, and sales and marketing professionals use LinkedIn as a tool to improve online corporate branding and develop new business. Similar to the approach used in *Windmill Networking: Maximizing LinkedIn*, *Maximizing LinkedIn for Sales and Social Media Marketing* provides information on all of LinkedIn's functionalities available for businesses to market their products, develop relationships that will help generate new business, and, ultimately, increase sales.

As you begin reading this book, please keep the following in mind: LinkedIn, as with social media websites in general, is always changing. Screenshots in this book may change on LinkedIn with no warning. Functionality that is explained in this book could be modified tomorrow. For this reason, please follow my Windmill Networking blog on social media strategy at http://windmillnetworking.com for the latest updates on LinkedIn and for additional information on utilizing social media for sales and social media marketing.

Before I jump into the heart of this book, I want to acknowledge all of those who have helped me create it. First and foremost, I need to thank my own family, headed by my lovely wife, Miwako, and my two children, Luna and Kyle, who have been extremely supportive of Daddy's crazy social media-infused work schedule. My parents, brothers, and sisters-in-law have also added their emotional support and wisdom over time to help me become a more focused and better writer. I have many friends to thank for their support, including old friends from high school James Wang, Eric Tom, Phil Ting, Todd Lieman, Cari Gilbert, and Julie Giventer (who is also my rock-star executive assistant) as well as friends from Amherst College Chip Galaty and John Beck. I appreciate the support the Alumni Office has offered as well.

As with most of us who are very involved in social media, our close friends over time include many whom we met through tweets, posts, and social events, and my support team here in Orange County and Southern California deserves special recognition (in alphabetical order): Hank Blank, Morgan Brown, Joel Don, Jeffrey Friend, Matthew Gallizzi, Ryon Harms, Greg Johnson, Gina Johnston, Phil Lauterjung, Glen Loock, Jack Molisani, Theresa Moretti, Norman Naylor, Ken Nicholas, Eva Smith, Tim Tyrell-Smith, Louise Marcelline Taylor, Robert Watson, Eva Wong, and Todd Zebert. A special thank you goes out to my ConnectOC team of Lara Gallagher, Marieke Hensel, Albert Ko, Debbie Miller, Ted Nguyen, Tanya Salcido, Dean Soto, Courtney Thurman, Paul Tran, Diana Wei, and Christine Weijland.

I also have a number of Windmill Networking "tribes" and social media fans that I've gotten to know throughout the country and even overseas. As you read this, I believe you already know who you are, but to you I say a big THANK YOU!

Although it may seem peculiar to thank my customers, they have believed in and given me the opportunity to showcase—and sometimes further develop—my skills, and for this I am indebted. I cannot name everyone who has provided assistance and support, but as you read this I hope you'll understand that I am deeply thankful for your investment in me.

This book is also an ode to the many sales managers I have had throughout my career who have provided me with the experience and intelligence to write a book of this caliber. I want to equally thank all of the professionals that have guided me to become a better sales person, sales manager, and, ultimately, business owner over the years, including Kiyoshima Mizushima (may your soul rest in peace) and Nob Hatta from Rohm Semiconductor; Rocky Chijiwa and Giuseppe Kobayashi from Wind River; and Derek South, Tom Siegel, Dave Williamson, and Jaison Dolvane from Espial. You have all helped shape who I am as a sales professional and for this I am most appreciative. It would be an honor if this book becomes one of your required reading assignments for sales training in whatever organization you may be working in now.

I would also like to acknowledge those LinkedIn employees who have engaged with me in a professional manner and understand that I am truly one of LinkedIn's biggest evangelizers. To you, I present this book in hopes that more businesses finally "see the light" and join the LinkedIn Revolution. It is my desire that this book also helps spark a mutually beneficial relationship between us.

Last but certainly not least, this book could not have been finished as quickly as it was nor without the quality that it represents without the help of my production team: My Lead Editor, JoAnna Haugen, who was well worth the flight to Las Vegas to meet and hire, has provided me with a wealth of expertise and experience that has helped guide the production of this book at every stage; my Copyeditor, Louise Julig, whom I never met before handing her my manuscript yet built a trustful relationship that included thoughtful guidance in the book process as well as introducing me to JoAnna; and my Graphic Designer Tanya Maiboroda, whose expertise added so much to the cover, formatting, and illustrations found in this book.

Introduction

AS YOU LOOK AT THE TITLE OF THIS BOOK, YOU MAY WONDER HOW ONE book could combine two distinctly different corporate disciplines.

It is true that, regardless of the company, people who work in sales and marketing are often separated into different departments, but it is their combined efforts and achievements that allow a company to become and stay profitable. Professionals in these two areas of business are essential in generating leads, developing prospective business, and closing deals, while small-business owners and entrepreneurs often have to take on both of these roles simultaneously.

With social customer relationship management (CRM) software, everybody in the company can gain access to the social media conversations of both present customers and decision makers for deals in the pipeline, and it is more important than ever that these two departments, which are responsible for a given company's revenue, work closely together. I have been responsible for the profit and loss for many organizations, and whenever the sales and marketing teams were in synch, everybody won, including our customers. Writing a book that can be used by both groups is a natural progression of social business.

Social media further blurs the line between sales and marketing because potential customers or new leads can interact with a social media profile that simply identifies a corporation rather than a single person in a particular department. Similarly, LinkedIn was not built for a specific discipline but is built on a unique platform that can accommodate business professionals who have a narrow work focus as well as those who work in many different capacities. For example, someone working in sales may find it worthwhile to use LinkedIn for gathering business intelligence and making contact with leads that are passed to them by the marketing department, while those in marketing might concentrate their efforts on generating discussions and leads in industry-specific LinkedIn Groups. Professionals representing small businesses or start-ups, or entrepreneurs who run businesses with extremely limited staff, may be using LinkedIn in a search for influential business partners who can help get them to the next level. Due to the interrelated nature of sales and marketing, it is important to understand how these two main outward-facing functions of a company can guide interactions on LinkedIn in a way that promotes the work of both the sales and marketing departments as well as the overarching mission of a particular company.

Though you'll interact as an individual with others on LinkedIn, there is an opportunity for your company to be represented on the site as well. In addition to addressing how to establish your personal credibility as a sales or business development professional on the site, this book provides information on how to establish a corporate marketing presence on LinkedIn (such as in Chapter 5 regarding companies pages and in Chapter 6 regarding groups). It's important to consider this hybrid approach because LinkedIn was originally created for professional networking by individuals, but there is an obvious advantage for companies that have both a corporate presence and an active employee presence on LinkedIn. Business is a fluid concept, and because so many positions require some crossover between sales and marketing—and because companies have a stake in having both departments represented online—it simply makes sense to address them both under the same cover.

I highly recommend that everyone read all sections of this book to better understand all aspects of the sales, marketing, and business development spectrum on LinkedIn. However, because this book addresses individual profiles as well as the corporate presence of enterprises, you may focus on those chapters that are most appropriate to your specific professional role in your company as follows, although all of the content will be relevant to small-business owners and solo practitioners:

- Chapters 1 and 2—Background information on the importance of social media in general, and LinkedIn specifically, for professionals [**everyone**]
- Chapters 3 and 4—Optimizing profiles and networks for individuals [**everyone**]
- Chapters 5 and 6—Establishing your company's LinkedIn Group and Companies Pages [**corporate marketing**]
- Chapters 7, 8, and 9—Developing business by engaging, prospecting, and utilizing business intelligence available on LinkedIn [**sales and business development**]
- Chapters 10, 11, and 12—Using LinkedIn to develop leads and attain thought leadership through participation, paid media, and social media optimization [**corporate marketing**]
- Chapters 13 and 14—Optimizing the LinkedIn presence through optional paid accounts and creating a daily routine for maximum efficiency and return on investment (ROI) [**everyone**]

If you are interested in learning more about LinkedIn and social media after reading this book, take a look at Appendix A, which provides additional online and print resources of interest. Case studies throughout the book and cataloged in Appendix B illustrate how professionals and corporations have used LinkedIn successfully, and will I hope provide inspiration for you and your employees, regardless of specific job functions.

The content presented in this book, along with this supplemental material, will equip the sales, marketing, and business development professionals at your company with new and creative ways to develop and foster business so that everyone can enjoy the success of maximizing LinkedIn.

The LinkedIn Mindset

CHAPTER OBJECTIVES

- *Understand how your online persona reflects your professional brand*
- *Differentiate between content that is appropriate for online professional interactions and that which is not*
- *Learn how to communicate messages that are aligned with your professional goals*
- *Appreciate that there are real people behind the virtual identities you meet online*

BEFORE I BEGIN EXPLAINING HOW COMPANIES AND PROFESSION-als can leverage LinkedIn for business purposes, I believe there is a certain mindset you should have in order to take advantage of the functionality and opportunities LinkedIn offers. Allow me to provide some personal experiences and insight that will hopefully put you in the right mindset to maximize LinkedIn.

Your Brand Is Your Online Persona

Whether you plan to use this book as an individual or to represent a business, you will be interacting with and be seen by others without having a chance to meet them. While corporate websites give us complete control over how we depict our brands, products, and personnel, LinkedIn levels the playing field by stripping away the design elements and simply presenting every user in basically the same way. Let me take this one step further and tell you that others may make decisions on whether or not they want to do business with you based on how you've utilized your LinkedIn profile.

An analogy that helps explain this has to do with business interactions I've had in Japan. I lived in Japan for 15 years, often representing foreign companies with little or no brand recognition in the market. When I went on a customer visit, therefore, everything I did represented not only my personal brand but also the brand aligned with my company. Did I take a *meishi* (business card) with two hands or one? At what angle did I bow when I was introduced? What was my body language when I presented to them? How quickly did I respond to their emails, and did I strive to use Japanese or fall back on my native English? All of these little activities added up to create a larger picture of who I was and how I did business, which then shaped how they viewed me as a person and eventually how they saw the company I represented.

This is exactly why social media, including LinkedIn, requires a strategic approach. Regardless of how much "branding" you try to include on your professional profile or company's page, your actions and words online speak much louder about you and your company than anything else.

You Are What You "Tweet"

In addition to your actions and words affecting your brand, you are what you tweet—a direct reference to posting a maximum 140-character message on the real-time social networking platform Twitter. If you are trying to generate business from other professionals, you need to stick to appropriate topics. There may be a time and place to talk about sports or family when you meet people in person, but on LinkedIn, these types of conversations are out of place and awkward. A professional's goal when using any form of social media should be to share content that his target customers find useful, allowing him to become the expert "channel" for that type of information. If you post useful and engaging comments that are aligned with your sales and marketing objectives, people will perceive you and your business as being skilled and experienced. However, if you clutter your message with off-topic comments, you run the risk of losing your credibility.

This concept holds true for status updates (or tweets, for those of you who have integrated them into your LinkedIn profile), discussions in LinkedIn Groups, and all other public avenues for communication that exist on LinkedIn. For instance, it might be tempting to chime in on a controversial subject that has been brought up in a LinkedIn Group or a disputed question on LinkedIn Answers, but due to the fact that anyone on LinkedIn—and, for answers and open groups, anyone on the Internet—can view your responses, you need to remember to communicate on brand.

When you create and display your profile, you must make public-facing decisions that communicate who you are as a person. Embedding a video and using a link that automatically plays when someone visits your profile may be a savvy Internet marketing tactic, but it may be perceived as a punch in the face to someone who just wants to check out your profile in order to potentially engage you in new business.

Treat LinkedIn with the same amount of respect you would treat a professional association meeting or industry convention and you will be on your way to building and enhancing your LinkedIn brand, which will be optimized for business success.

Creating a Public Persona

When you see the value of communicating on brand or in a way that is aligned with your professional objectives for being on LinkedIn, you'll likely sense the need to create a "public persona" of yourself. In other words, avoid posting your private information on LinkedIn, and all social media in general. Did you know there are tools, such as a plugin for Gmail called Rapportive[1] and the social CRM platform Nimble (shown in Figure 1.1 on the following page),[2] which can be used to publicly display available information for every email address with a registered social media profile?

1. http://rapportive.com
2. http://www.nimble.com

FIGURE 1.1   My Public Persona (as shown on the social CRM platform Nimble)

If you're not careful with your Facebook profile, for example, your private information could cost you potential business.

The fascinating thing about social media, of which LinkedIn is definitely a part, is the social component. It is what draws some people into having conversations and posting things on various social media channels that they might later regret. It is very possible for this to happen on LinkedIn. Consider the fact that LinkedIn allows you to input information about your hobbies and interests in your public profile. Including this information may help make a connection with a potential customer, but it may also turn off potential customers who perceive you in an unintended manner.

The overarching problem is that everyone sees and uses social media from a different perspective. A statement that is considered harmless by some may be perceived differently by others. When Kenneth Cole tweeted in the midst of the 2011 Egyptian revolution, "Millions are in uproar in #Cairo. Rumor is they heard our new spring collection is now available online…,"[3] some of his fans didn't think twice about the message. However, because of the public nature of Twitter, within a few hours of the tweet, there were complaints via Twitter and even blog posts talking about how insensitive the tweet was. Shortly thereafter, Kenneth offered an apology via his Facebook page, but that didn't stop the tweet from being broadcast on national news that night…and printed in this book.

It's easy to say that in creating your public persona you should avoid putting certain things in your profile, but because social media is, well, social, we're frequently tempted to say things that may catch us off our public brand. Before you post something in any social media channel that may be controversial and therefore affect your future business prospects, ask yourself the following four questions:

Would my family approve of this?
Would my boss approve of this?
Would all of my customers approve of this?
Would a court of law approve of this?

Unless you can answer "yes" to all four of these questions, keep your public persona intact by simply not posting your opinions on the Internet.

---

3. http://wind.mn/kencole

Building Virtual Networks Online

The final thing to remember about public personas is that there is a real person behind every photo and profile on LinkedIn. It is easy to browse through hundreds of profiles and treat them as mere numbers, but the fact is that these profiles represent professionals from across the entire American and global spectrum. These are people with whom you want to create mutually beneficial and long-lasting relationships. Because social media was made for people and not for businesses, this will require you to network with, instead of market to, people, in order to generate business. If you can understand this concept, you can use LinkedIn to create a hyper-targeted and global network of professionals in a way that is much easier online than offline. Online networking requires you to socialize in a different way than you do offline, but real, valuable relationships can be created through LinkedIn.

I started becoming a heavy LinkedIn user in early 2008 when I was looking for new professional opportunities. I had been a member since 2004 and understood its potential value for sales and marketing, but after living in Japan and moving back to a new location in my native United States, I realized that my network had minimal reach in my new locale. LinkedIn, and thereafter Twitter and Facebook, became my tools of choice to develop and expand my professional network. The people in my network continue to support me by providing recommendations for services that my business needs to grow as well as introducing potential clients to me. I also appreciate knowing that, wherever I travel around the world, there is a small network of LinkedIn connections that I can tap for whatever business networking needs I might have.

While some people choose to keep their LinkedIn connections confined to those they know personally (which is in line with LinkedIn's current User Agreement which states, "Don't invite people you do not know to join your network"[4]), the people you connect with outside of your established networking circle may become your most valuable business contacts.

---

4. http://www.linkedin.com/static?key=user_agreement

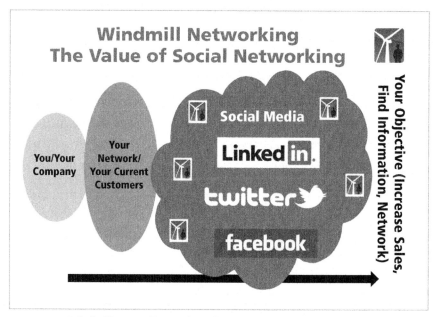

FIGURE 1.2 *Windmill Networking—The Value in Building Out Virtual Networks through Social Media*

Many networkers I meet agree that the value of networking is in meeting new people. Armed with a well-crafted public persona and the ability to look at LinkedIn as a networking tool for business (rather than personal) purposes, I am confident that you, too, can make virtual connections of value on LinkedIn that will help your sales, business development, and marketing efforts.

With this mindset in place, you will be able to increase your chances of developing business on LinkedIn specifically and in social media in general.

LinkedIn User Advice: "LinkedIn is only valuable if you decide to be an active member."

When I reached out to a number of companies and professionals who had developed business using LinkedIn, I was struck by the recommendation of James A. Rohde,[5] a market research consultant based in Pittsburgh,

---

5. http://www.jamesarohde.com

Pennsylvania. Here's his advice, in his own words, on the LinkedIn mindset.

"I recently started my own research consulting firm and have been lucky enough to develop business clientele mostly by relying on LinkedIn. Based on what I've found so far, the network has been amazingly valuable, though only when used the 'right' way. LinkedIn is a great public forum to see what issues people are trying to solve, which has obvious benefits when your job is to sell solutions. That being said, I have never opened and closed a prospective deal by relying just on LinkedIn. It is simply a valuable tool in a larger set.

"LinkedIn is built on the idea that there is power in knowing the 'degree' of your relationships with other professionals. The value of the system when it comes to selling is in understanding that this philosophy works both ways. By presenting the benefits and philosophy of your services to an open forum of people who can trace you back through their own connections, this bolsters an initial trust that is not obtained through traditional advertisements or even the more traditional conferences (in the B2B world).

"LinkedIn is only valuable if you decide to be an active member. At least for me, the success I've had with the networking site has stemmed from participating in conversations and providing honest and real opinions to the topic at hand.

"My overall feeling is that LinkedIn allows more people to take comments and conversations seriously because everybody has their professional reputations on the line. Discussions are being held by more than just random names; they are held by people working at specific companies that also employ two or three other people you worked with in the past."

Why Every Business
Needs to Be on LinkedIn

CHAPTER OBJECTIVES

▪ *Understand why representation and engagement on LinkedIn is essential for any business*

▪ *Appreciate the differences between what LinkedIn and Facebook can offer businesses*

▪ *Learn how a company's employees can utilize LinkedIn to develop their sales and marketing skills and value*

BY NOW YOU PROBABLY KNOW THAT LINKEDIN IS THE PREMIER social networking site that is devoted solely to professionals. While you might find some profiles set up by college students when doing a search, an overwhelming majority of users are professionals. In fact, LinkedIn's 100 million members include an executive from every Fortune 500 Company.[6] This means there is no other social networking site where you have a greater chance of being able to interact with an influential decision maker.

Though many social media marketers concentrate their efforts on Facebook or Twitter, LinkedIn remains the best social networking site to market your business-to-business (B2B) products and services because

---

6. http://press.linkedin.com/about/

of this special demographic. LinkedIn is also important for business-to-consumer (B2C) companies; not only are wealthy consumers members of LinkedIn (the average LinkedIn user has an annual income over $100,000,[7] a statement no other social networking site has claimed to date), but also B2C companies have B2B marketing initiatives that involve distributors, partners, and strategic alliances.

The Job-Seeker Misconception

Ranking	Industry
1	Information Technology & Service
2	Financial Services
3	Computer Software
4	Education Management
5	Telecommunications
6	Hospital & Health Care
7	Higher Education
8	Banking
9	Real Estate
10	Construction
11	Marketing & Advertising
12	Retail
13	Government Administration
14	Insurance
15	Accounting

FIGURE 2.1 *Top 15 Industries Represented on LinkedIn (according to LinkedIn Ads, April 5, 2011)*

If you think LinkedIn is just for job seekers and recruiters, you are missing out on an important business opportunity. A look at the top 15 industries represented on LinkedIn (shown in Figure 2.1) reveals that, even with the combined number of users who categorize their profiles under human resources or staffing and recruitment, these industries do not make the list. Based on this statistic, recruiters make up only about one percent of all LinkedIn users, which means that the majority of networking done on LinkedIn is not related to job searches at all.

7. http://blog.linkedin.com/2007/12/18/top-10-ways-for/

If you're still not convinced that LinkedIn offers value for your company, I'd ask you to consider these points on why representation and engagement on LinkedIn is critical for any business:

LINKEDIN PROFILES AND COMPANIES PAGES ARE FREE YELLOW PAGES. Many businesses and professionals are using LinkedIn as they would the phone book, looking for experienced, qualified, and recommended service providers, businesses, and professionals. When someone needs insight or information about your industry, is your company or sales personnel being found? And if they are found, can non-paying LinkedIn members easily contact them?

NO OTHER TOOL MAKES IT AS EASY TO CONNECT TO DECISION MAKERS. Search, find, and ask for an introduction. To simplify the process, LinkedIn gives you tools to conveniently facilitate this every step of the way. Considering how easy it is to network with others on LinkedIn, you may wonder what business development professionals did before its creation.

YOU CAN GAIN MINDSHARE WITH POTENTIAL CUSTOMERS. Companies invest in search engine optimization (SEO) and search engine marketing to help potential customers find them online, and they use email marketing to help gain mindshare with clients on a regular basis. With the time, effort, and money spent to reach potential and current customers, it only makes sense to maintain a presence on LinkedIn, which is currently the 16th most visited website in the world,[8] so that your company, products, and employees are the hot topics in your industry.

LINKEDIN HAS BECOME AN INCREASINGLY IMPORTANT SOURCE OF BUSINESS INTELLIGENCE. With so many professionals having so many conversations and sharing so much information about themselves via their profiles on LinkedIn, platforms such as LinkedIn Companies and

---

8. http://www.alexa.com/siteinfo/linkedin.com

applications such as LinkedIn Signal are now providing a unique source of business intelligence for free, some of which cannot even be found on paid services such as Hoovers or OneSource.

LinkedIn vs. Facebook: Which Is Right for Your Company?

Early in my social media consulting career, I received a request for a proposal from a niche B2B software company. The director of marketing stated that her company had already started utilizing social media, and when I asked what they had done, she mentioned that they had created a Facebook Fan Page. *Sigh.*

Successful social media marketing is about knowing where your customers are and establishing a presence there. It is clear that professionals from all demographics are spending a great deal of time with social media, and that Facebook is the main networking site where we spend—or waste—our time. However, simply because many people are on Facebook doesn't mean it's the best use of time and effort for businesses. If you asked most people what they use certain social networking channels for, they would likely say that Facebook is for private use and LinkedIn is for business. That is, most people—including the decision makers with whom you want to connect—use Facebook to keep in touch with friends and family. LinkedIn, on the other hand, is viewed by professionals as a trusted place to network. Not only is the perceived purpose of each site different, but so is the demographic; many more-experienced professionals are not represented on Facebook, and those that are don't engage on fan pages as much. LinkedIn may have fewer users, but the professional mindset and ability to network with other people who are on the site for the same reason makes LinkedIn a much more valuable tool for B2B companies than Facebook.

Admittedly, there are many similarities between Facebook and LinkedIn. For example, both Facebook and LinkedIn offer platforms so that people can become a part of a business' community. On Facebook these are called fan pages, and on LinkedIn these are called companies pages. Facebook Fan Pages allow people to interact via wall postings while LinkedIn Companies

Pages allow professionals to recommend company products and services as well as add comments to their recommendations. LinkedIn followers can see who in their network made what company recommendations just as Facebook users can see which of their friends like certain pages. LinkedIn has a widget that allows anyone to recommend your products and services on LinkedIn from any website, which is similar to Facebook Social Plugins.

However, a closer comparison of the two platforms demonstrates how LinkedIn provides better B2B business opportunities than Facebook:

LINKEDIN ALLOWS FOR MORE TARGETED PROFESSIONAL COMMUNITY-BUILDING. Just as you can create an ad on Facebook prompting consumers to "like" your page, similar ads on LinkedIn beckon professionals to "recommend" products and services. Above and beyond recommending a business, though, LinkedIn's feature to follow a company allows you to "like" it simply by following it. As a result, these follower numbers have grown over time and companies such as Hewlett-Packard have (at the time of writing this book) amassed more than 285,000 followers.[9] Compare this to the 315,000 fans HP's Facebook Page[10] has. Though the LinkedIn Companies Page for HP has slightly fewer followers than its Facebook Fan Page, those following the LinkedIn page are much more relevant to the business aspect of the company simply due to the professional demographic of LinkedIn.

LINKEDIN ALLOWS FOR MORE ROBUST INTERACTION BETWEEN COMPANIES AND FOLLOWERS. On Facebook, businesses are fairly restricted to fan pages, but LinkedIn offers the ability to build a public community of professionals with LinkedIn Groups in addition to the company page functionality. (Groups will be explained in more detail in Chapter 6.) Having a LinkedIn Group offers distinct advantages over a Facebook Fan Page; content from the outside world, including your website, can be shared directly in LinkedIn Groups with the LinkedIn share button, which can now be easily embedded into websites just as Twitter's

9. http://www.linkedin.com/company/hewlett-packard
10. http://www.facebook.com/HP

retweet and Facebook's share buttons are. LinkedIn's button is the more comprehensive feature, however, because it allows you to *simultaneously* share website content on your profile as well as directly to LinkedIn Groups.

LINKEDIN OFFERS BETTER PAGE MANAGEMENT TOOLS. Many Facebook Fan Page administrators have problems managing their pages efficiently because settings don't allow for specific content control. However, LinkedIn has several moderation tools built into the groups that allow for granular detail regarding who can post what. For instance, the process for LinkedIn Group administrators to search through members, see when they joined the group, add them as managers, delete them, or delete and block them is simple. Facebook does not offer this extensive collection of features. In this respect, LinkedIn Groups are at the cutting edge of community management on any major social media site.

PUBLIC ACCESS ALLOWS FOR GREATER ENGAGEMENT WITH INTERESTED PEOPLE AND INCREASED VISIBILITY. Up until recently, Facebook Fan Pages had been *the* open arena in which people could engage. Previously, the problem with LinkedIn Groups was that they were private worlds; unless you were a member of that group, you couldn't see inside it. The openness of Facebook Pages and the associated potential SEO benefits attracted companies to create pages and send more advertising revenue to Facebook. However, LinkedIn recently began to allow existing groups to become public and new public-only groups to be created.

It's worth noting that the largest LinkedIn Group at the time this book was written, Job Openings, Job Leads and Job Connections!,[11] had more than 450,000 members, while Facebook's own page[12] had more than 46 million fans. However, the *number* of LinkedIn Groups (more than 960,000[13]) was not that far behind that of the 1.3 million+ Facebook Pages.[14] As more of

11. http://www.linkedin.com/groups/Job-Openings-Job-Leads-Job-1976445
12. http://www.facebook.com/facebook
13. http://www.linkedin.com/groupsDirectory?results=&keywords=
14. http://www.socialbakers.com/facebook-pages/

the legacy LinkedIn Groups go public, they will flood the search engines with enough content to rival that of Facebook in due time. An increasing number of group discussions will come up in long tail search results, which will drive more traffic to LinkedIn and result in higher membership numbers in groups. Now that Facebook Fan Pages and public LinkedIn Groups offer virtually the same benefits regarding SEO and visibility, there is little reason for companies *not* to be active on LinkedIn.

GROUP MEMBERS ARE ALLOWED MORE ROOM FOR IN-DEPTH CONVER-SATION. The engagement on LinkedIn Groups is significant because there is a lot of room for discussion; users are not confined to small status update boxes such as those used on Facebook. Furthermore, LinkedIn Groups offer daily and weekly digests so that followers can stay on top of discussions through email, a feature lacking with Facebook Pages.

The fact that you invested in this book means you already understand the sales and marketing potential of the LinkedIn platform and demographic. In 2011, we are already seeing signs that many marketers, especially those in B2B industries, are starting to realize this. A recent report indicated that B2B marketers use LinkedIn more than Facebook for marketing as well as for socializing.[15] There is no question that for an increasing number of companies, LinkedIn is the preferred social media channel for business. LinkedIn's recent initial public offering will only increase the number of businesses and professionals flocking to and utilizing its platform.

LinkedIn as the Virtual Industry Event of the Year...24/7

Now that we've established how LinkedIn can assist you and your company, it's important to note that utilizing it effectively to develop business for your company in a social networking environment is not an easy task. Traditional Internet marketing methods such as sending out a lot of invites

---

15. http://wind.mn/bizreport0404711

CASE STUDY

**Utilizing LinkedIn Groups Versus Facebook
Fan Pages for Business Purposes**

While speaking about the difference between LinkedIn and Facebook, I was happy to learn about a B2C company that realized LinkedIn was a good supplement to its Facebook strategy. This company, like many, realized that, while its consumers were on Facebook, its business partners were on LinkedIn—and these potential business partners are open to being "sold to" as long as you provide them value.

BACKGROUND

Kelly Ducey and her husband own the popular and quickly growing Irish Dog Bloody Mary Mix,[1] located in Moline, Illinois. Irish Dog is a gluten-free, secret family recipe that they perfected and made by request for family and friends for years. They discovered there was a wider market for the product, however, so Ducey and her husband went into business 15 months ago, and, in that time, they have sold just over 55,000 bottles and grown from one Hy-Vee food store distributor in Moline to 25 distributors across 17 states. The couple has primarily used progressive and innovative social media marketing efforts to grow the business and pick up new distributors, states, and fans. As part of this strategy, Ducey and her husband have joined groups on LinkedIn and posted newsworthy updates sparking interest from customers and new distributors.

They made a very conscious choice to concentrate their efforts on LinkedIn rather than solely working with Facebook. "In my experience (of) using both Facebook and LinkedIn, people don't like to be 'sold' on Facebook," Ducey said. "It's more of a social interaction site where people like to be a part of something." That is, people on Facebook like to be updated on company happenings, involved in socializing with others who use a particular product, and kept in the loop on events and promotions, but they aren't interested in a sales pitch. As a more business-oriented site, LinkedIn is the better place for this type of interaction. In addition, LinkedIn allows business owners to target

---

1. http://www.drinkirishdog.com

distributors or people in certain markets within the groups. "Facebook limits you to your already-existing fans unless you want to place an ad, which wasn't right for us," Ducey said. "Facebook allows us to target our consumers. However, LinkedIn allows us to target the companies and distributors who would be picking up or wholesaling our product to the consumers."

WHAT HAPPENED

Ducey signed up for several LinkedIn Groups that were specific to her company's industry or product, such as Beverage Executives USA, Spirits & Liquors, Wine and Spirits Professionals, and F&B Professionals, and posted newsworthy tidbits about Irish Dog. "My initial postings were something like, 'Quickly growing Bloody Mary company seeking distributors nationwide. Visit www.drinkirishdog.com for more info!'" Ducey said. "I would post and then get several emails from people interested in learning more or wanting to sample or carry our product. I sent out a lot of free product from those postings—and still do—and gained three of our initial distributors that way through LinkedIn for the entire states of Missouri, Texas, and Colorado."

Active participation in these LinkedIn Groups also greatly spread awareness about Irish Dog. After the company gained some distributors and started expanding into other states, Ducey posted updates such as, 'Irish Dog is now in eight states after our first year in business,' or, 'Irish Dog is now in 18 states in a year and a half,' which also got a lot of response. She also posted updates in her typical groups as well as on several beer sites after the company won its first award in September 2010 when it partnered with Budweiser. These posts received several responses as well as interest from distributors who wanted to sample and carry the product. "My postings also generate some online orders from consumers, and many have turned into raving fans that have reordered many times since there are no distributors in their areas yet," Ducey said.

After gaining distributors in certain markets, Ducey also joined groups that applied to those markets, such as LinkedAtlanta, and let people know that the award-winning Irish Dog product was now available in their area. "Basically, I just keep people updated with mini press releases each time we have something newsworthy to post," said Ducey. "Most recently, I posted about our partnership with Brown Dog Foundation and that a portion of each bottle of Irish Dog sold is donated to Brown Dog. I also joined some pet-friendly groups to target those people who would really appreciate our partnership with Brown Dog."

SUMMARY

Ducey and her husband have found that when they are active on LinkedIn, it generates up to 27 percent of their website traffic. More importantly, the distributors they found via LinkedIn currently represent 25 percent of their business.

to key targets and opting them into mailing lists will be met with LinkedIn account restrictions and a plethora of spam reports back to your email provider. But if we think about LinkedIn as a virtual trade show, we can see the types of opportunities available. Instead of waiting for your annual industry trade show or even monthly chamber of commerce meeting, check to see if the people you would connect with in person are active on the LinkedIn platform. This virtual trade show is happening 24 hours a day, seven days a week, and it is a truly global event with membership from more than 200 countries. Don't you want to market your company at this ultimate event?

Every Employee Can Be a Sales Person

If you wanted to attend a trade show that was several time zones away, you might not send every person from your sales, marketing, and business development organization because of budgetary concerns. And yet, if you could attend a trade show with all of your staff, wouldn't that increase your chances of success at the event? With LinkedIn, everybody can join and participate for free. It is this same logic that dictates that every employee with a revenue-generating aspect to their position should be on LinkedIn and utilizing it as a cost-effective marketing tool.

The way to get your employees on LinkedIn is to lead by example. If the top person in your company organization is not an advocate of LinkedIn, unable to lead by example, or unwilling to educate others on how to utilize it as a tool, it may be a difficult internal sale. It's also vital that LinkedIn is open and available for your employees to use during business hours. In order to drive home the importance of this business device, share stories with your employees and educate them about how you have closed business deals or received invaluable introductions utilizing LinkedIn. This allows your sales and marketing employees to envision how LinkedIn can be used as a tool in their respective roles.

It should be in every sales and marketing employee's best interest to have a LinkedIn membership and be active on the site. However, it is also important to understand the law and how utilizing social media relates to your industry. If your company does not have an internal social media policy, it is best to consult with an employment law firm to understand the potential implications of requesting your employees to utilize LinkedIn as part of their job.

Get Your LinkedIn
Profile In Order

CHAPTER OBJECTIVES

- *Understand why all employees in your business should fully engage on LinkedIn*
- *Learn how to create the most complete sales and marketing profile*
- *Clarify how LinkedIn views completed profiles and why that matters*
- *Learn how to take your LinkedIn profile beyond completeness with optimization*

N ORDER TO MAXIMIZE YOUR COMPANY'S EXPOSURE ON LINKEDIN, it's important to realize that you aren't the only person who needs to take professional networking seriously. Every sales and marketing employee that represents your business needs to have a LinkedIn profile as well, and everyone in the company needs to take the time to clearly and comprehensively complete it.

Getting Your Company's Network Connected: Why Every Sales and Marketing Employee Should Have a LinkedIn Profile

Though you want your company to be found on LinkedIn, the networking doesn't stop there. Because LinkedIn is a social networking platform, many people seek out those with expertise by doing a keyword search under "People." This means every employee representing your company that is on LinkedIn increases the chances that your company will indirectly be found, and the more connected your employees are to others (including each other), the easier it will be for those wanting to contact any of your company employees to do so through the LinkedIn platform. This is one of the main reasons why your sales and marketing employees should have complete and accurate profiles that highlight their skills and spotlight your company.

The LinkedIn search algorithm has changed over the last several months and the number of connections you have does not affect standard search results, but there is a chance that people will search and sort the results by "relationship," meaning first-degree connections come first, followed by second- and third-degree connections. There is a function in LinkedIn that allows you to be introduced to people that are connected with your first-degree connections, but it can be difficult to reach third-degree connections. Because free members of LinkedIn only receive 100 search results at a time, you want to ensure that as many of your employees as possible show up as high as possible in the relationship rankings for any given keyword that is associated with your company. (The process for connecting with second- and third-degree connections is covered more thoroughly in Chapter 4.)

In addition to filling out complete profiles, you and your employees must upload your professional contact databases to LinkedIn in order to maximize the number of people from your company that appear in search results. This is obviously a personal decision and your employees may react adversely to the request to relinquish their business contacts, but as professionals, our network of customers, clients, and other connections from the past are key assets we bring to any organization we might join in the future. LinkedIn makes it easy to connect with past classmates and colleagues, and if you make an effort to keep and foster those relationships, the stronger your entire organization's network is on LinkedIn. It goes without saying, then, that sales and marketing professionals in your business who stay connected on LinkedIn will help your company's chances of being found as first- or second-degree connections in any given search term.

Creating Your Sales-Oriented LinkedIn Profile

Now that we've established why it is important for all sales and marketing employees in your organization to be represented on LinkedIn on behalf of your company through the use of professional profiles, it's time to dissect the main functions of a profile and explain how each component can be used. There are several sections of the LinkedIn profile that can be filled out, but instead of offering a thorough look at what to do with each of these as I have in "Windmill Networking: Maximizing LinkedIn," I want to concentrate on those areas of your profile that are especially important for successful sales and marketing development for you as an individual as well as your company. The LinkedIn profile is the public-facing summary of who you are, what you represent, what your professional history is, and your areas of expertise. Your profile is, in essence, a snapshot of the brand you are sharing with the entire world.

When you establish your profile in a way that highlights your company's expertise and outlines how you can assist potential customers, you maximize the business opportunities for you and your business. Although you might customize the way in which you present your company in each business interaction, there is only one universal profile on LinkedIn that everyone will be able to see. This is the secret to why LinkedIn's database and people search capabilities are so impressive: The fields in which everyone enters information are standardized. For this reason, it is easier to brand yourself with your profile because everyone else has to complete the same data fields as you do. By doing something different you will undoubtedly make yourself more noticeable if and when someone visits your profile.

One of the reasons why it is important to set up a proper profile has to do with inbound marketing of yourself and your company. You want to attract attention to your profile, which means you want your profile to come up high on the first page of search results for related keywords within LinkedIn when others are looking for someone with expertise that you and your company can provide. However, those searching for you don't see your full profile; they first see what limited information is included for your profile in the search results, and those things most prominently shown are your photo, name, and professional headline. One of the primary objectives in optimizing your LinkedIn profile is to have someone choose your profile from several search results, and that selection often comes down to these three elements.

In creating your LinkedIn profile, it is also important to consider potential engagement with a customer or client. If your abbreviated profile interests people and they actually visit your comprehensive profile to see if they want to develop a relationship with you, your profile should reflect what they found in the search listings. The same photo and professional headline are also here, but now the summary, which appears near the top of your profile, becomes important, and everything below it should back up and ideally enhance your profile.

How much information should you put in your profile? To develop and strengthen your own LinkedIn brand and increase your chances of being found, you want to include as much data as possible. I will only cover the minimum of what I recommend you have on your profile, but once you create it, you don't need to waste any more time on it, except for maybe a brief monthly or quarterly review to ensure that it still represents you and your company. Spending time on creating the perfect profile now means you won't have to worry about it later, and it also allows you to move on to other areas of LinkedIn that will help your business prospects.

With that in mind, let's examine the ten most important parts of your profile and how you should complete them. If you already have a profile on LinkedIn, simply choose the "edit profile" option under the "profile" section to make any adjustments. To see how others view your profile, select "view profile" under the same profile section.

1. Your Photo

Not adding a photo to your profile was the first thing I touched on when I wrote about this issue in my now-viral blog post, "LinkedIn Profile Tips: The 10 Mistakes You Want to Avoid and Why,"[16] and for good reason. If you don't have a photo on your profile, you are invisible. Don't forget that

---

16. http://wind.mn/liprofiletips

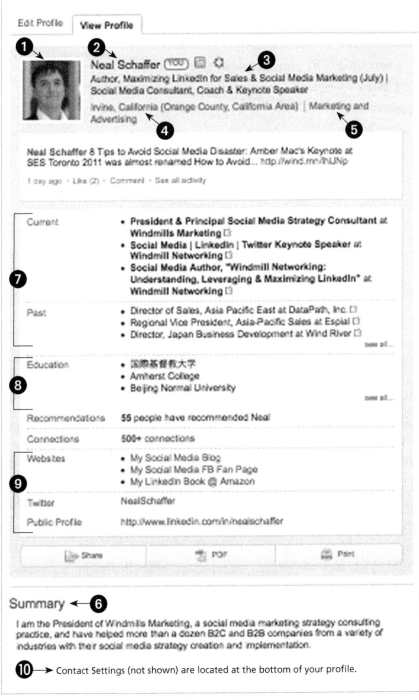

FIGURE 3.1   *Ten Most Important Parts of Your Profile*

the heart of LinkedIn, and much of social media, is about people-centric networking. Without a photo of yourself, you really don't exist, and this will make it harder to gain credibility with those whom you want to engage.

There used to be some debate as to whether or not you should include your photo in your LinkedIn profile, but there are many fundamental reasons why you need to upload a photo to your profile if you haven't done so already:

- There are fake profiles on LinkedIn. A photograph shows that you are real, which helps establish your social media credibility.
- Why would you be on a social networking site and not display who you are? Not posting a photograph on your profile may turn others off from pursuing business with you. People are much more likely to contact you if they can put a face with the name.
- Not displaying your photo may raise suspicion in the minds of potential clients.
- As a sales professional, a photograph is essential. As they say, first impressions mean everything, and often our first impression is a visual one.

There is also a debate, since LinkedIn is a site for professionals, about what type of photo you should post. You definitely do not want to post a potentially embarrassing photo, such as those you might upload to Facebook for friends and family to view. Some people post more professional photos, like those you would see on corporate website bios, and others choose to post those that include children, family members, or friends. This is really a personal choice; it comes down to how you want to portray yourself to the outside world according to your own professional objective. The market you target or type of business you represent will help determine what type of photo is most appropriate. I believe the golden rule in photo selection is that your choice of clothing should be what you would wear in the presence of your client's or potential customer's CEO.

Note that there is no mention here of displaying a corporate logo in lieu of your own photograph. Based on the above logic, a logo will not help in establishing credibility for yourself or your company.

People do business with people they trust. Your photo is the first step in obtaining trust from someone who has never had the chance to meet you.

2. Name

LinkedIn is strict when asking you to input your name, and only your name, where specified. If you have a maiden name or a nickname by which you are commonly known, including them here will only help increase your discoverability if someone is searching for you. Obviously you do not want to include a company name or add something to the end of your name to advertise something; there are plenty of other places where you can do this. You will see many people who continue to use something other than their name in this space, such as if I called myself Neal "Social Media" Schaffer, but should you need to contact LinkedIn's customer service department for something, they will not help you if your proper name is not shown on your profile.

Furthermore, it just looks unprofessional. It's like attending a networking meeting wearing your company t-shirt and a badge advertising your product. Blatantly changing your name is truly as "in your face" as you can get, and I don't mean that in a positive way. People will continue to do this because of the potential SEO benefits of including keywords, but there are other ways of optimizing your profile, which I will discuss later in this chapter.

It should also be noted that, though you have the option to show only the first initial of your last name, unless you have something to hide, you should join the majority of members who include their entire names. LinkedIn gives you this option for privacy purposes, but, quite honestly, with the reach of social media today, if you're online, your life isn't private. Having an online presence without revealing who you are has the potential of turning people off from looking deeper into your profile.

Finally, if you are representing a business and want to use your company's name for the profile, keep in mind that LinkedIn is a social network for professionals and people, not companies. There are plenty of opportunities to brand your company within your profile. Profiles that have company names in place of actual names go against the LinkedIn User Agreement and may be deleted.

3. Headline

Your headline is the important real estate that appears next to your name in search results, and its wording may determine whether a new potential client contacts you. Don't just put your company name and title here; your headline should be customized to align with your objective for being on LinkedIn in the first place, which is to market your company. For instance, if you are in charge of a particular type of product, genre, or market, put those details instead of your company name and official title here. Give your potential visitors some context regarding why you would be the appropriate person to contact if they have an interest in working with your company.

There is also a branding side to the headline. After all, with the exception of your name, it is the part of your profile that will receive the most visibility (though it is limited to 120 characters), so think carefully about how you want to brand yourself here. This may be the appropriate place to include your key branding statement, or you can add information about your profession and indicate your objective for being on LinkedIn. Enter searchable keywords to increase your visibility. If you're not sure what to include, LinkedIn provides some generic examples, and it can also help to search for others who may have similar objectives or professional backgrounds for headline inspiration. Simply search for others in your industry with similar titles and see what they include in their headlines for ideas.

One last reminder: Make sure you use as many of the characters that LinkedIn gives you as possible to maximize the potential for branding your headline…and therefore appearing in more LinkedIn search results.

4. Location (Country/ZIP Code)

While the country/ZIP code field may seem like a no-brainer, take a moment to think about what to put here. This is the field that gives potential customers a way to filter out profiles by location, so it is of the utmost importance that you classify yourself as "living" where your market is. Let me give an example here: I live in Orange County, California. I look for service providers close to my ZIP code. I only contact those that display "Orange County, California" on their profiles in search results. Let's say you live in Los Angeles County but actually have your office in Orange County. What ZIP code are you using for your LinkedIn profile? If you are not using the ZIP code where your business is located, you are misrepresenting yourself…and missing out on my potential business.

Here is another example: You live in Connecticut, have a desk at your headquarters in New York City, but actually sell to a territory where your biggest market is in Central New Jersey. Wouldn't it make more sense to use a ZIP code that gives you the appearance of being close to, rather than far away from, your market?

It should be noted that, for those of you worried about your privacy, LinkedIn takes your privacy seriously. If you decide that the ZIP code of where you live is more appropriate for this section, you should know that the actual city name of where you live, based on your ZIP code, is not displayed and only your closest major metropolitan area appears. The ZIP code you enter is merely used in searches when trying to locate someone, or some service, a certain number of miles away from your address.

5. Industry

This is another critical aspect of your LinkedIn profile that you need to think about. It's a tricky question because you are being asked to compartmentalize yourself into a silo called an "industry." Many of us might work for a company that represents multiple industries, or you could be responsible for developing business in an industry in which your company wants to launch a new business. Just as you want to pick the ZIP code where a majority of your business is, you need to do the same with your industry. Needless to say, if you don't have a "territory" and work at corporate headquarters, you'll want to pick the industry that closest represents your company.

What should you do if there is no clear, singular answer regarding the industry your company represents? Many sales and marketing professionals struggle with this because your company's industry is not always clear.

I have looked at several profiles of employees from my previous company, and, interestingly enough, people's choices regarding the industry they selected varied. Whichever industry you choose, it is very important to pick one that you want to be associated with, as this will be a key field upon which searches could be based.

In trying to decide what industry to choose, it might help to look at what other sales and marketing professionals in your company—and in competing companies—choose. What it ultimately comes down to is imagining what industry your target customer might choose; that's the industry you should select.

I'd like to offer one final example on why choosing the proper industry is essential; if I am looking for a bookkeeper, I will likely search the "accounting" industry. Perhaps you are a bookkeeper and want to upsell your consulting services so you choose "financial services" or "management consultant" for your industry. As a result of your choice, I will never find you, and you will not receive my business. Remember, you only get the leads aligned with your industry, even if you offer exactly what your potential clients want.

6. Summary

Your headline acts as an initial filter when someone views your profile, and your summary is the basis upon which people will form opinions about you and your brand.

Should people navigate to your profile after selecting your name from a search result, the summary is what helps them decide how they will view you and potentially your company. This is your chance to tell the world who you, and even your company, are. It is the part of your profile that can play up your brand because of its prominent location and the large area of text you are given. You can copy and paste your bio from your corporate website if you are an executive, or you can go into more detail about your professional background by detailing your expertise in the industry, products, or discipline about which you hope customers will contact you.

Although employees, not employers, own LinkedIn profiles, you can potentially help your sales and marketing staff by creating a keyword-optimized template paragraph about your company that can be used as part of the summary. This can't be forced upon your employees, but they will probably consider using it if it helps them achieve their goals in your company.

Notice that there is also a "specialties" section that appears under the summary. My advice is to fill this space with keywords you want associated with your profile. In the past, I have broken up these keywords into industry-specific and skill-specific paragraphs, but regardless of how you organize this section, any important industry, product, or other keywords that do not fit naturally into your summary text should be included here.

Because this is such an important part of your profile, it's worth repeating the rule of thumb for data entry: If there is a keyword with which you want to be associated when people conduct a search, make sure you have included it in your summary, as this is the most suitable place for it.

7. Experience

Even after the robust summary area is filled in, LinkedIn gives sales and marketing professionals yet another chance to promote themselves and their companies in the experience section. Not only can you list the companies and job titles you currently have and previously had, you can also write about your experiences and areas of expertise at each company. I am always surprised when I find business owners who don't take advantage of this space to write about their experiences, products, and service benefits in keyword-rich terms. This is your opportunity to show off your company's niche and your own unique expertise.

As you start adding your professional experience, your current position is what will appear at the top of your work profile. Your current position also appears within the search results, so it is essential that you list the firm that you currently represent. Follow your current work experience with details about your previous experiences including company name, title, dates worked, and a description of your position. Since potential clients will see the description, don't be shy when listing your responsibilities at your current company as well as how you can help potential clients. To effectively brand yourself, you will need to include details that support the information you included in your profile's headline. This is not a carbon copy of your résumé. Rather, you need to show off both your company's and your personal professional achievements in enough detail to entice someone to contact you and others representing your company.

LinkedIn gives you the option to add several positions in this profile section, and there doesn't appear be a limit on how many you can add. Because your profile is a sales and marketing tool and not a résumé, it works to your advantage to list all relevant past positions. Make it as discoverable, approachable, and accessible as possible. Furthermore, what you deem as work experience (which may be unrelated to what you currently do) may actually be the experience that one of your potential clients needs. Maximize this section of your LinkedIn profile by including as many past companies and professional experiences as you feel comfortable.

8. Education

Despite the fact that many people skip over this section of the LinkedIn profile, you should not. Education is another way to prove you are "real." This is especially important if you work in an industry where a college degree is important. Skimping on this section may mean that potential leads will not contact you simply because you don't meet their educational standards. Filling out this section also gives people—specifically those that are alumni at the same school—one more reason to get in touch with you. People you may have met in classes, during extracurricular activities, or at parties may now be the decision makers at companies you'd like to target.

When entering your educational background, don't stop with your university or master's/Ph.D. program. If LinkedIn is about finding and being found, it makes sense to also list your high school as well as any other foreign institutions you may have attended during your college years. To add a school, begin typing the name of the institution in the box that asks for the school name. A dropdown box will appear as you begin typing. Choose your school from this list if it is available; if it isn't, type in the name of your school in its entirety. There are also fields to enter your degree, field(s) of study, dates attended, activities and societies, and additional notes. For most professionals, there is no need to enter activities and societies, but there are a couple of cases where this can be helpful. For example, if you were involved in an organization that strengthens your professional brand, such as serving as the chair of the Public Relations Student Society of America at your university, this helps to further showcase your expertise and leadership abilities.

9. Websites and Public Profile URLs

I am always shocked by how many service providers do not include a link to their company website on their LinkedIn profile. Don't make potential customers dig for information about your company, because most people aren't going to waste time doing so.

Not only do you have the opportunity to list your company website, but you can list up to three URLs to appear on your profile. Take advantage of this by listing the URL for your main product or a special landing page for visitors from LinkedIn. Note that you can also customize the text label description or anchor text of each URL site that you enter. Use this to your benefit and help your target URLs become more search engine optimized.

You should also be aware that every profile comes with a default public profile URL, which is automatically assigned to you, that will lead non-LinkedIn members to your profile. Do yourself a favor: Edit this and claim your personalized URL now. If you are the first one to claim your name, your public profile URL will be easy to remember (www.linkedin.com/in/YourName). Include this as part of your email signature or on your business card to drive more traffic to your profile and achieve a connection with any new professionals you meet.

10. Contact Settings

LinkedIn has a spot at the bottom of your profile for contact settings. Most people leave it blank, but this is the area where you can and should share your guidelines for being contacted. If you are open to being contacted by potential clients, or you actively want to create certain types of professional relationships, let people know that in this section. If you want to keep your network closed and don't want to receive invitations from virtual networkers, this is the place to say so.

You will often see email addresses and phone numbers noted here as well as in other sections on LinkedIn. The rationale is easy to understand; if you're representing a business, and your business is listed in the telephone directory, would you only show your name and city? Of course you wouldn't. Make it easy for potential clients to contact you by inputting contact information here. If you don't want to show your phone number, a business email address is sufficient. Do not leave this area blank.

There is a section on the LinkedIn profile above the contact settings called personal information that allows you to input fields including your phone number and address. You can enter information here, but, in addition to your contact details, consider including advice on how best to contact you, what times are best to reach out, and when and how people can expect a response.

Listing your email address in your profile comes with an inherent risk. There are companies that actually "scrape" LinkedIn profiles for email addresses, so you might be inviting spam into your inbox. On the other hand, if potential clients want to get in touch with you and can't because your contact information is not readily available on your profile, you run the risk of losing them to competitors who took the chance and posted this information in a place that was easily accessible on LinkedIn. Consider it this way; if you're looking for business, don't you want to make yourself approachable?

The same logic goes for your phone number. If you are hesitant about listing your phone number for privacy reasons, perhaps this story will change your mind. I joined a certain LinkedIn Group, and the very next day I received a call on my cell phone from someone trying to sell me a service related to that group. I was shocked that someone who didn't know me had found my cell number, and when I asked how he had gotten it, he said he had called the company listed as my current employer and asked for me. The point is this; anyone who wants to contact you for the wrong reasons will find a way to do so, so you might as well list your phone number on your profile anyway in order to make it easier for potential clients to contact you.

At this point, I'd like to offer one last word of advice. After you create a stellar profile that embodies your LinkedIn brand, make sure you revisit it on a regular basis to ensure it is up to date and still reflects your professional objectives. There are many reasons why your profile might need to be revisited—perhaps you begin working for a new company or your present role has you changing your target industry—so remember to maintain your profile so your LinkedIn brand is always fresh and up to date.

Creating a "Complete" Profile

LinkedIn gives you a lot of real estate with which to work, so the more you use, the better you can brand yourself and your company, making it easier to be found in LinkedIn's search results. This means you should add a paragraph and/or at least a few bullet points listing all of your education and work experience.

Profile completeness is in the eye of the beholder, but LinkedIn provides a way for you to measure how thorough your profile is. As you edit your LinkedIn profile, a gauge at the top right-hand side of the page indicates your profile completeness on a percentage scale. If you follow my ten tips above and enter at least two companies that you currently or previously worked at, all it will take is three recommendations for you to reach 100 percent completeness.[17]

Although I just gave you advice on a sales-centric approach to completing your LinkedIn profile, let's take a step back and make sure that you've truly done everything you can to make your profile as comprehensive as possible. If you filled out your profile according to the advice above, you are well on your way to having a "complete" profile, but there are still a few missing pieces displayed on your profile that aren't actually a part of what technically defines a completed profile. These include having a recent status update, securing recommendations, and making connections. True

---

17. http://www.linkedin.com/static?key=pop%2Fpop_more_profile_completeness

CASE STUDY

How Prospects Find You through Your Profile

Business is found on LinkedIn every day, and opportunity abounds for those found in LinkedIn searches. How does this work? Let me tell you the story of how I hired a service provider through the power of a LinkedIn search, which also illustrates some of the points covered in this chapter.

BACKGROUND

Before my first book was published, I decided that it would be a good investment to apply for a trademark on my "Windmill Networking" brand and logo. When professionals and businesses look for a company to solve a business problem they have, they often turn to their networks to find a recommendation for assistance, and this is what I did in this situation. Unfortunately, despite having one high school friend who is now a patent attorney at a large telecommunications company, there was no lawyer that lived near me that anyone was able to recommend.

Where could I to go to find someone to help? The phone book? Google? Nope. Why would I go to these places when, on LinkedIn, I can see people's photos, read their bios, see where they went to school and worked, and read recommendations from those in their trusted network? LinkedIn profiles provide the background data needed to make a purchasing decision that can't be found through traditional search methods of the phone book, a newspaper, a magazine, or even search engines.

I referred to LinkedIn as a great place to build a "trusted network of advisors" in *Windmill Networking: Maximizing LinkedIn,* and, in my present situation, I realized that I needed to supplement my network by utilizing LinkedIn and adding a business partner to my team. This was not the first time I had done this, and I am sure it won't be the last, but I also believe this is how many businesses will use LinkedIn as the "new" Yellow Pages going forward.

WHAT HAPPENED

Here is the process I followed, which should shed some light on how potential clients may search for you:

- I did a search for "trademark lawyer" and confined my search to within 50 miles of where I lived using the advanced people search.
- My search did not yield any first-degree connections. However, there were a number of second-degree connections that appeared in the first page of the search results.
- I contacted the first five second-degree connections that met the following criteria:
  - ☐ Their profiles had enough professional information (photo, description, etc.) to be seen as being reputable.
  - ☐ They had multiple recommendations on their profiles.
  - ☐ I was able to easily contact them for a variety reasons: They had their contact information in their contact settings, they had a link to their website in the public profile URL section, we were members of the same group, or they were an OpenLink member (to be discussed in further detail in Chapter 13).
- Of the five lawyers I contacted, I had phone interviews with the first three that responded. For me, responsiveness was very important, particularly because I never had a chance to personally meet these people in advance. This indicated that these people were real and open for business.

One week later, I hired my new trademark lawyer, who confided in me that it was the first time he had developed business from his LinkedIn profile. I'm sure it won't be the last.

SUMMARY

A LinkedIn profile needs relevance (keywords) and credibility (recommendations, detailed information) as much as it needs approachability and ease of contact. However, only your sales skills will help you close the deal, so never forget to be responsive to any social media lead.

LinkedIn profile completeness (according to my definition below) increases the chances that your business will get new leads from LinkedIn.

Redefining LinkedIn Profile Completeness

My definition of a completed profile differs from LinkedIn's definition. This is because I base my reasoning on how clients might look for you as well as how your professional branding might be perceived by them. In order to create the most complete profile, I suggest you take action in the following areas, some of which were covered in depth earlier in this chapter:

1. **List your full name.**

2. **Display your photo.**

3. **Have a professional headline that properly brands you.**

4. **Have something relevant and timely in your status update.**

    The status update appears on your profile as a white box next to your photo. You enter content for this area on your LinkedIn home page in the box that prompts you to "share an update." I will cover this in more detail in Chapter 7, but it's worth noting briefly how this space should and should not be used. I see many people simply linking to their status updates on Twitter, but you should not utilize this tool to broadcast tweets that may be irrelevant to your network. In addition, the status update area is not about gaining mindshare by constantly blasting your network with your network updates.

    Instead, use the status update to show you are still relevant and active in your area of expertise. Are you going to an event or attending a conference? Share that information with your network. Did you read something interesting that might interest your customers? Tell them about it in this space. It's best to use your status update to show your relevance; make an effort to update this part of your profile at least once a week. (What to include in a status update will be covered in depth in Chapter 7.) Don't let this status update go stale; always keep something fresh in this area.

5. Display enough work experience…and include details.

6. Show off your alma mater.

7. Get recommendations.

I don't think there's any magic number of recommendations you need to have in order to achieve a complete profile. My suggestion is that you get at least one recommendation for every position that you've had, preferably from the manager to whom you reported. The ultimate goal is to get a sound bite from someone who can vouch for your authenticity and professionalism. Having recommendations also validates your brand. I mean this in all seriousness. Chances are you've been in business for several years and you have happy clients to whom you refer potential customers. If this is the case, there is no reason not to have LinkedIn recommendations. According to the LinkedIn completeness algorithm, unless you have three recommendations, your profile does not show up as being 100 percent complete, so this is another reason why every sales and marketing professional should have at least three LinkedIn recommendations.

8. Acquire connections.

If you're on LinkedIn, you should be networking. If you are a professional, you should have several years of legitimate experience from which to cultivate potential connections. The calculation is easy; all things being equal, the older you are, the larger your network should be. Don't forget to connect with friends in other professions and people you met in college (both professors and colleagues) as well. Connections also help make your profile more visible in the massive LinkedIn database. Chapter 4 will provide extensive information on how to increase your number of connections.

9. Complete your professional summary.

10. Include your contact information.

LinkedIn Profile Optimization

The SEO industry is estimated to be valued at more than 15 billion dollars.[18] Companies want to ensure that their websites and products are found when consumers or potential clients conduct searches on Google and other search engines. Since LinkedIn has its own search engine and you're using this social networking site to market your company and help your employees be found, you should invest time in optimizing your LinkedIn profile for successful SEO. As indicated earlier in this chapter, LinkedIn provides plenty of opportunities to place keywords in your profile, but now it's time to leverage this function to increase your firm's LinkedIn SEO.

A primary aspect of inbound marketing on LinkedIn is making sure that you and your employees appear in any given LinkedIn people search by optimizing the keywords in their profiles. Just as Google changes its search algorithm regularly, the same is true for LinkedIn, and it is best not to think of any magic formula that will give you the top search results for any given keyword. That said, LinkedIn is a real-time search engine, so by changing keywords in your profile, you can quickly test how you perform compared to the competition. But just like Google search results, your "competition" is a moving landscape, so it's best not to dwell too long on this issue.

Is there a chance that LinkedIn could start penalizing people that stuff keywords in their profiles? Will LinkedIn penalize profiles that are updated too often by not allowing them to appear in search results? Both of these could potentially happen as LinkedIn matures, but it's hard to say for sure. With that in mind, I suggest you ensure that your main keywords appear in each of the following areas of your LinkedIn profile and move on: headline, summary, specialties, and experience (at your current company).

You might want to consider creating a standard keyword-optimized description of your company that your employees can voluntarily use in their profiles to help them with their individual inbound marketing.

For those who are curious and want to achieve the very best results for any given keyword, my advice is to do a keyword search and take a look at where your preferred keywords appear in the profiles that appear in the top

---

18. http://wind.mn/sysox

ten search results. This will also allow you to see how some professionals "dupe" the LinkedIn search engine by using the following tactics:

- Including the keyword as part of your name
- Including the keyword multiple times in your headline
- Including the keyword in your LinkedIn profile's URL
- Having the keyword in your integrated Twitter account
- Repeating the keyword multiple times in your summary and specialties sections
- Repeating the keyword as part of your title as well as in your descriptions for multiple companies at which you presently work
- Repeating the keyword as part of your title as well as in your descriptions for companies for which you have previously worked
- Including keywords in sections such as interests, honors and awards, groups and associations, and education

This list is not meant to guarantee you any given search result, but if you want to experiment with keyword optimization, the above should provide you with a lead on where keywords seem to have search algorithm value. While prudent use of keywords can help improve your SEO and strengthen your professional brand, using it in your name and awkwardly repeating the same phrase can potentially damage your branding. When emphasizing the SEO of your LinkedIn profile, tread carefully.

How Do Your Company Employees Rank?

One easy way to confirm the success of LinkedIn profile optimization efforts your company has put forth is to see how you rank for any given combination of search terms. Figure out your top markets by ZIP code as well as the industry filters your potential clients might use to find your company's sales and business development staff; then test those keywords your potential clients might use and see if any of your employees appear near the top of the search results.

CASE STUDY

How Profile Keyword Selection Yields Business

If someone is looking for your specific expertise, it is vital that they be able to find you easily. When you create your LinkedIn Profile, take the time to ensure it adequately and accurately details everything about you that a potential client might want to know. By optimizing your profile, you run a higher chance of being found when someone goes looking for a person that fits your description.

BACKGROUND

An independent financial reporting & consolidation consultant, Martin van Wunnik[1] was constantly on the search for projects in order to make a living. In order to maximize his time on LinkedIn, he had to create a profile that was written not from a job seeker's perspective but was designed more like a curriculum vitae and listed all of his previous experiences.

WHAT HAPPENED

Van Wunnik was contacted on a Monday by a UK-based agency via an email address listed on his own website (which was noted on his LinkedIn profile) for a project in Brussels, Belgium, the country in which he lives and mainly works. Van Wunnik later found out the agency discovered and contacted him specifically because the term "consolidation" appeared in his profile, and his geographical location met the agency's needs. On Tuesday, van Wunnik interviewed with the Belgian client, at a meeting organized by the agency, and by Wednesday he was offered the project contract. He began work the following week.

SUMMARY

This business deal turned into a seven-month contract project for van Wunnik, and it resulted in half of his yearly turnover in 2010. Because he continues to seek out consultant projects, he frequently revisits his profile and ensures it is up to date. So should you.

---

1. http://www.arsimaprojects.eu

If you commonly track your website search engine results by keyword, you might want to look at where you rank using the LinkedIn people search engine as well and track it over time. Doing so will also help your company stay up to date on the latest trends of the LinkedIn search algorithm as well as ensure you are maximizing your key employees' profile optimization.

If some of your sales and marketing employees have paid account plans, you can further supplement this information with the top keywords that LinkedIn users use to find them as noted in the Profile Stats Pro application (discussed in more detail in Chapter 13).

Reestablishing Your LinkedIn Network

CHAPTER OBJECTIVES

■ *Understand the importance of reaching out to connections beyond your immediate network*

■ *Demonstrate the importance of constantly checking for new network connections*

■ *Provide guidance on how many connections you should have in your LinkedIn network*

BUSINESS HAS BEEN AND ALWAYS WILL BE ABOUT PEOPLE conducting business with each other, not companies conducting business with each other. For many companies, a majority of business comes from repeat customers as well as the ability to create a referral engine from these loyal customers. (If you are interested in learning more about this topic, I recommend you read "The Referral Engine: Teaching Your Business to Market Itself" by John Jantsch.)[19] Companies receive referrals from their extended network, which includes partners, strategic alliances, and even personal connections. LinkedIn fosters referral networking. Establishing a strong LinkedIn network with a robust profile and client recommendations will naturally bring you more referrals over time.

---

19. http://wind.mn/ducttapereferral

It seems logical that people would be interested in creating a large and strong network on LinkedIn, but for some, this is not the case. Many users say they only want to connect with people in their closed network, but unless that network is big enough, the benefits of using LinkedIn to find and be found are minimal. In fact, from a sales and marketing perspective, it is almost counterintuitive to keep a small and closed network on such a valuable site. If you haven't opened up your network beyond those people you actually know, it's time to rethink your policy on networking, stop taking social media too personally, and start leveraging the power of LinkedIn.

LinkedIn is a database that helps you and your company be found if people are looking for you, but if you don't have enough connections, you aren't going to be found nearly as often as you could be if you had a more open network. As noted in the previous chapter, your professional network should include a long list of people who include former classmates, former and current colleagues, business partners, past and current clients, personal friends, family members, and just about anyone else with whom you've come in professional contact.

It concerns me when I see a sales and marketing professional, or worse yet, a business owner, on LinkedIn with only a few connections. It raises questions regarding their legitimacy in the business and their commitment to make and foster relationships in a very people-driven business world. A lack of connections also casts a shadow of doubt on how trustworthy they, their brands, and their businesses are. People who signed up for a LinkedIn account and forgot about it would be better off deleting their profiles, because an inactive profile only works *against* them and is, quite honestly, a form of negative advertising. Maximize or delete; there is no middle road in social media.

I assume you know how to add connections on LinkedIn, but when in doubt, simply press the "add connections" link that appears prominently on the top right-hand corner of any LinkedIn screen. If you haven't gone through this exercise in the past few months, you owe yourself a favor to do it again for the following reasons:

LINKEDIN NOW HAS MORE THAN 100 MILLION MEMBERS.[20] In June of 2010, LinkedIn only had 70 million members,[21] so in less than one year, the number of LinkedIn users has grown by almost 50 percent. In fact, one million new members now join LinkedIn every week.[22] This means that a lot of professionals in your network who didn't appear when you uploaded your contact database in 2010 may now be active LinkedIn users. If you search for professionals from past or present companies or your college again, you are bound to find someone you know among these newer members. Add them to your LinkedIn network. The site makes it particularly easy to find colleagues and classmates because it shows you when you last searched and conveniently introduces you to only those new people who did not appear in your previous search.

LINKEDIN HAS INCREASED SUPPORT FOR ADDITIONAL METHODS OF FINDING YOUR NETWORK. At the time of this book writing, LinkedIn supported 39 different email providers. In the past you needed an email account with AOL, Hotmail, Yahoo, or Google, but now you can upload your email contacts from domains such as att.net and mac.com as well as a host of international domains.

YOU MAY KNOW MORE PEOPLE THAN YOU THINK. As your connections grow, so do those of your network. There may be other professionals you know that you somehow forgot to connect with, but the improved "people you may know" feature will help you find more professionals with whom you have many common connections.

How Many Connections Should I Have?

You don't need to have a lot of connections to be effective at networking on LinkedIn. In fact, while those with more connections used to appear in more search results or were even ranked in search results based on how many

20. http://blog.linkedin.com/2011/03/22/linkedin-100-million/
21. http://wind.mn/techcrunchli70
22. http://press.linkedin.com/148/linkedin-create-100-new-jobs-dublin

CASE STUDY

Developing Business through the Art of Connecting

Generating or developing leads often arises from a single data point such as a lead passed from a marketing partner, a phone inquiry, or perhaps a response to an email newsletter that is sent out for the purpose of maintaining mindshare. Sending out LinkedIn invitations to your network serves the exact same purpose; it is another data point that may provide a spark of engagement that just might lead to new business.

BACKGROUND

This is my favorite success story from a series of interviews that LinkedIn used to publish on its blog. This is culled from an interview with a particular LinkedIn user.[1] As with many of us who joined LinkedIn early in its creation who thought that receiving invitations to connect was more of a nuisance than an opportunity for business growth, this person really didn't do much with his LinkedIn account. Then one day after starting his own consulting company, he decided to get connected with his network through LinkedIn.

WHAT HAPPENED

This LinkedIn user uploaded his contact database in order to connect with his professional network on LinkedIn. He sent out a personalized invitation letting his former colleagues and friends know that he had just started a consulting firm, but he also let them know that he valued their connections and wanted to carry the relationship over to LinkedIn.

A number of people responded to his invitation, including one who was a former client. This particular person wanted to know more about his company, and that communication sparked what would become a million dollar deal for him. As he said with a smile during his interview with LinkedIn, "Not bad for a fifteen-minute investment of time."

1. http://blog.linkedin.com/2008/10/09/reconnecting-wi/

SUMMARY

As professionals, our networks are our most important assets. Once we are connected with those we know, we can leverage our relationships every time we encounter a new prospect on LinkedIn. Sometimes the simple action of sending an invitation provides the data point we needed that catapults into a new beneficial idea—or even new business.

connections they had, this is no longer the case. Whether you have made no connections or are an open networker with 25,000, you will appear in the same number of search results, but if someone sorts the search results by connections, the order in which you appear might be different.

With this in mind, the number of connections is now irrelevant to how you appear in LinkedIn searches; however, having LinkedIn connections makes you appear approachable, credible, and active on the site.

The question then becomes how many LinkedIn connections should you have?

Everyone's network size and participation on LinkedIn will be the result of several varying factors. My rule of thumb regarding connections is, multiply your age by ten to give you the minimum number of connections you should have. I also recommend that you set a reasonable goal of meeting and potentially linking up with ten to 20 new people each year through networking events. Even if you're fresh out of college with few professional connections, I believe the calculation that I propose is reasonable. If you're a true Windmill Networker, you can easily meet ten to 20 new people in a month or even a week! In fact, I have attended networking events where I meet several people I want to connect with in a single *day*.

Creating Your LinkedIn Connection Policy

As a sales and marketing professional, you are probably trying to decide how to move forward with growing your LinkedIn network. If you've been a closed networker in the past, you're probably wrestling with this quandary; should I continue with my previous policy of only inviting those whom I know and trust, or should I open up my network and utilize my LinkedIn connections as a tool to help extend my reach and aid my inbound marketing?

At the end of the day, LinkedIn is a business tool. It has a number of applications that allow us to share, discuss, and engage with each other, but when it comes down to it, it is simply a database of professional profiles. Just as you should optimize your profile so the proper keywords can be found, you should increase your network size in order to aid in your discoverability as well.

There obviously is no single right or wrong answer here, but as this book is about helping you maximize LinkedIn for sales and marketing, let's look at the pros and cons of extending your reach on LinkedIn to people you've never met in person:

Pros

- More connections mean potentially increased business networking opportunities from new first-degree connections if they are relevant to your business objective.
- More first-degree connections mean that there are more second-degree connections from which you are only one introduction removed. More second-degree connections mean that you will also appear to be only one connection away from more people in search results.
- More third-degree connections adds to your general discoverability and approachability on LinkedIn

Cons

- Opens up the potential to receiving more spam and communication that you did not opt in to beyond connecting on LinkedIn.
- You may feel uncomfortable receiving introduction or recommendation requests from people you have never met before.
- You do not want to expose your network of trusted professionals to those for whom you cannot personally vouch.

I have personally gone from being a very closed to a very open networker on LinkedIn and now have more than 26,000 connections. As a result, I can speak to the disadvantages based on my experience and, if you are concerned about becoming an open networker, I would advise that you consider the following; there is definitely a potential to receive more spam, but whenever you join a webinar, sign up for a free e-book, or even join a LinkedIn Group, you inherently open yourself up to receiving communication you didn't expect to receive. Spam has become an unfortunate way of life in the digital age. To combat this issue, I immediately unsubscribe from mailing lists to which I did not subscribe, report them as spam to the email-marketing provider, and report the spam back to the ISP through my email provider.

The hesitation to follow through on introduction or recommendation requests for those you don't know is a valid one, and I rarely pass them on to people I personally know unless I feel they might be genuinely interested. This does not defeat the purpose of making the connection, however, because the simple act of opening your network at least provides the potential to create a genuine business connection.

It's also important to realize that building an open network is a bit like paying it forward. I find that it's common for a connection I don't know to contact me for an introduction to another person on LinkedIn I am connected to but don't know. In such a situation, I let the person who requested the introduction know that I made it, and I let the receiver of the introduction know that he is free to act upon the request as he wishes, but if I can be of any help, I let him know that as well. It's a simple introduction to make, both parties are often happy about it, and I've made myself known as a valuable connection.

If you choose to become an open networker but are fearful of allowing others to see your connections, you can control who gets to view this section of your profile. Do this by hovering over your name in the top right-hand corner and selecting "settings." From there, navigate to "profile" and then "select who can see your connections" under the privacy controls column. If one of your open connections does a search for people, someone in your network appears, and you appear as the one who connects the two, you may be pinged for an introduction request, but you do not have to actually make the introduction.

Open networkers may want to consider one other thing in defining their LinkedIn connection policy; there are certain types of profiles that you will probably want to avoid because they are clearly fake or they are trying to get you to buy into something. These profiles often have one or several of the following characteristics:

- No profile photo
- Keyword stuffed names which often include phone numbers and/or email addresses
- Sales-oriented profile headlines and summaries
- No "current" position
- The "current" position and what is stated in the headline conflict with each other
- Nothing in the profile except for the current position and headline

The creation and maintenance of a LinkedIn connection policy is critical because, as you and your business become more active on LinkedIn, you will organically receive more invitation requests. As a sales and marketing professional, you need to spend time with your customers instead of debating whether to accept invitations to connect on LinkedIn. Whether you decide to use LinkedIn for a personal reason or utilize it for its sales and marketing potential is up to you, but you should create a connection policy, put it into play, and then reap the benefits that result from whatever choice you've made.

It's Not About Your First-Degree Connections!

Figure 4.1 illustrates how a robust personal network (my own) quickly grows through a succession of first-, second-, and third-degree contacts. With every first-degree connection you make, your second- and third-degree connections, by extension, grow at a rapid rate. In fact, you don't

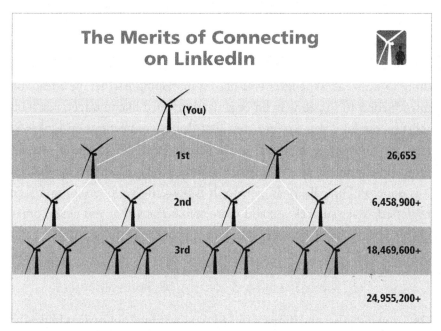

FIGURE 4.1   *My LinkedIn Network in Numbers*

need to be an open networker to achieve as many as one million second-degree connections from only a few hundred well-connected first-degree contacts, and, quite honestly, it's your second-degree connections that are most critical in your network.

Why don't first-degree connections mean as much as second-degree connections? The value and therefore the business opportunities in networking happen when you connect with people *outside* of your network. This is because your first-degree connections already know about you and your business, and so, in most scenarios, no business can be gained simply by connecting with them on LinkedIn. It's when they connect you to their connections or vice versa that business opportunities occur. Yes, you need first-degree connections to increase your second-degree reach, but you don't need a lot of first-degree connections to build a sizeable network of second-degree connections on LinkedIn. Once you've created a well-connected, solid base of first-degree connections, you are only one introduction request away from hundreds of thousands, if not millions, of professionals. All of those people are also only one introduction away from you as well.

It is one thing to build an extensive network, but it's an entirely different thing to utilize it. Whenever you need a marketing partner, new lead, or introduction to someone in an organization you'd like to target, you'll be most successful if you tap into your first-degree connections on LinkedIn and ask for that warm lead. Introductions and the resulting mutual professional value is the very essence of networking, regardless of whether it is done on LinkedIn or in person. It is powerful yet often forgotten or neglected. Make sure, as you add more connections, that you never forget nor underestimate the power and value of your LinkedIn network.

Connecting with People Outside of Your Network

Once you move beyond the generic "add connections" option that LinkedIn has, you might want to specifically search for and increase your connections with people aligned with your LinkedIn connection policy. The challenge is that restrictions exist within LinkedIn that may prevent you from inviting others you don't personally know. You are entitled to try to connect with people without knowing their email addresses, but once five people respond to your invitation to connect by noting that they don't know you, your ability to connect will be restricted by LinkedIn.

You will want to connect with new people in accordance with your LinkedIn connection policy, but let's look at some specific scenarios you might encounter that could affect how you attempt to connect with them:

- You're a product marketer interested in investigating a new market in which you have no connections.
- You are charged with developing business in a new market where you don't have any professional connections.
- You joined a company as the new sales representative and are responsible for a client where you only know one person. This person is the gatekeeper who doesn't like your company, and you are looking for additional contacts in order to navigate around him or her.

In each of the above scenarios, a new, targeted LinkedIn connection could potentially provide you with the guidance you need to make the necessary connections.

Once you've decided you want—or need—to connect with new professionals, chances are you will initially find them by doing advanced searches for people. If you are already an experienced LinkedIn user, you'll likely encounter people you might want to connect with everywhere on LinkedIn. These people often show up on the omnipresent "people you may know" widget that is featured prominently in the top right-hand corner of your LinkedIn home page and in group discussions. They are the people who respond to LinkedIn Questions and "like" blog posts published on LinkedIn Today. Chapter 7 discusses how best to engage with other LinkedIn users in each of these applications and more, but suffice to say there are several ways to "meet" new people on LinkedIn.

Once you find someone with whom you'd like to connect, follow these guidelines to complete the connection:

1. Read the contact settings.

There are many people on LinkedIn who aren't engaged with LinkedIn. They signed up and forgot about their profiles, or they simply "checked out" for some reason. Some may indicate in their contact settings that they are not open to receiving connections, but if they include their contact details here or anywhere on their profiles, you have implicit permission to contact them. If you want to be cautious, first contact them and let them know why you want to connect. Also mention how you can help them. Then ask if you can connect on LinkedIn for a mutually beneficial—and connected—relationship.

2. "Read" the profile.

A LinkedIn profile says a thousand things about someone's attitude toward online professional networking. Consider these two fictitious profiles:

Person A

Person A doesn't have a photo on his profile. He has a simple headline and only shows the most recent company for which he worked, and, even then, only displays his title and the name of the company with no summary. He has only a few connections, is not a member of any groups, has no recommendations, and doesn't provide any information in his contact settings.

Person B

Person B has a well-developed profile with a summary as well as job descriptions completely filled for every company at which she has worked. She has more than 500 connections and a few recommendations, and she is a member of several groups.

Although these might seem like two extreme examples, the point is that just by perusing a LinkedIn profile, you can determine how active a particular LinkedIn user is. In general, the more active people are on LinkedIn, the more they understand the value of business networking and thus the more willing they will be to connect if you send a personalized invite.

3. Warm leads are always the best.

As in real life, a "warm" lead, someone your target connection actually knows who can make a personal introduction on your behalf, often leads to the greatest success. Rather than relying on a cold call or email, get in touch with the person who connects the two of you and ask him or her for a formal introduction. Better yet, indicate specifically how you'd like to be introduced. Make it as easy as possible for your first-degree connection to introduce you, and you will have a much better chance of actually succeeding in making the new connection. Online or off, the rules for business introductions still apply, so don't forget to maintain professionalism throughout this entire process.

If your targeted user is a third-degree connection, find someone who could facilitate an introduction between you and a person who is actually connected to your targeted user. Your eventual goal is to be introduced to your second-degree connection who can then facilitate the introduction with your third-degree connection. Because this can be a complicated string of events, don't feel as if you need to use the LinkedIn introduction request feature for this. It may help to take the conversation offline and foster your professional network elsewhere to make the connection you need.

4. Don't forget your manners.

Just as you should continue to foster warm leads in the "real" world, you need to do the same online. Don't forget that, behind every online persona, there is a real person. Whenever you communicate with someone online, you should personalize your communication and give him or her reason to connect to you. Answer the question of what is in the relationship for your new connection. Though LinkedIn doesn't provide much space for personalizing your invitations, a little personalization can go a long way. Always remember that manners apply online just as they do offline, and LinkedIn (as with all social media) is simply an example of utilizing new tools, old rules.

5. Join the same LinkedIn Group or send the "Hail Mary" InMail.

A simple tactic you can use to contact someone is to join one of his or her LinkedIn Groups. Of course, this only works if your desired contact has the default settings on, which allows group members to send messages to each other. At present, the option to send a message to a group member does not appear as an option when you find a common group member on an advanced people search result; instead, you will be prompted to send an InMail. However, if you share a group with your desired contact, simply navigate to that group and search for his or her name in the Members tab. When navigating your cursor over the name in the search results, there should be a notation in the top right-hand corner of the profile that indicates that you can send a message instead of sending an InMail.

This brings us to the mighty InMail, a paid LinkedIn service to contact people who are not first-degree connections, which I consider to be the equivalent of a Hail Mary toss in a football game. LinkedIn promotes the use of InMail as being a very effective way to communicate on LinkedIn,[23] but if someone has already disengaged from LinkedIn, sending an InMail will likely be in vain. However, if the person you want to connect with is active but simply doesn't join groups or is a member of groups that you cannot join, then sending an InMail does give you credibility because it indicates that you paid for the privilege to contact him or her. (Rest easy if you are concerned about the expense: LinkedIn will refund you an InMail credit and allow you to send an additional InMail should the person you'd like to contact not respond within seven days.)

At the time of writing this book, LinkedIn has finally allowed non-paying members the option to purchase InMails à la carte for $10 apiece. Though some people might shirk at the idea of paying for such a service, consider it a business investment that *may* result in future professional opportunities. Everyone's experience will be different, so you should at least experiment with the InMail and determine your own ROI.

Strategically Expanding Your Network

Depending on your LinkedIn connection policy, it might be time to explore how to strategically expand your network. Here is a simple exercise that should result in finding several profiles you might want to approach for an introduction or connection via an invitation.

Conduct the following advanced people searches, but make sure you sort by connections, which you can set in the dropdown box at the very bottom of the screen. This allows the results to be shown by those users with the most connections in decreasing order. The number of LinkedIn connections people have is the best and easiest indicator you can use to determine how active they are on LinkedIn, and if they appear to be particularly active, they'll potentially be more open to connecting with you. More connections naturally means a greater chance they can help connect you with professionals in your target market.

---

23. http://www.linkedin.com/static?key=about_inmail

- Search within ten miles of your target market's most central ZIP code without using any keyword. ➡ Connecting with someone here will expand your local reach in the community where your customers are.
- Search within ten miles of where you live without using any keyword. ➡ Connecting with someone here will expand your local reach in your own community.
- Search your industry, using the location option of "anywhere" without using any keyword. ➡ Connecting with someone here will expand your reach within your own industry.
- Search your client by entering the company name in the company field without using any keyword. ➡ Connecting with someone here will expand your reach within your client's organization.
- Search your college alumni by entering your college name in the school field without using any keyword. ➡ Connecting with someone here will expand your reach within your own alumni organization on LinkedIn.

By doing the above searches you are bound to find many professionals who might be able to help you reach your sales and marketing LinkedIn objectives. Don't forget to do your due diligence before blindly sending out invitations though, and make sure you keep your online persona intact by personalizing your outreach efforts.

Creating Your Business Outpost on LinkedIn Companies

CHAPTER OBJECTIVES

▦ *Learn how to set up and maximize the functionalities on a LinkedIn Companies Page*

▦ *Understand the difference between LinkedIn's Companies Pages and Facebook's Fan Pages*

▦ *Learn how to integrate social media marketing into your company's page*

▦ *Appreciate the importance of engaging the followers of your company's page*

N ORDER FOR YOUR SALES AND MARKETING TEAM TO GET THE MOST out of inbound marketing on LinkedIn, your company must be cataloged in the LinkedIn Companies directory. LinkedIn Companies, which was launched in 2008, is a database comprising information that is primarily user-generated as well as extracted from information held by LinkedIn partners Capital IQ and BusinessWeek. Due to its backing from these major firms, LinkedIn Companies is quickly becoming an alternative free source of company information, and, in fact, LinkedIn claims that there are more than two million company profiles on LinkedIn Companies.[24] That alone should be reason enough to ensure your company is listed.

The information provided in LinkedIn Companies is a hybrid between data that companies can control and user-generated content from LinkedIn

---

24. http://press.linkedin.com/about/

users who work at a particular company. From a marketing perspective, it makes sense to establish and optimize your company's presence on LinkedIn with a company page in order to exploit any free advertising opportunities that LinkedIn provides. In addition, the LinkedIn Companies functionality offers marketers the chance to improve reputation management and create a community of "followers" to capitalize on in the future. For sales and business development professionals, LinkedIn's Companies Pages offer business intelligence that can be used to monitor present clients, target customers, and other LinkedIn users that may, in some way, provide assistance to your company some day.

Understanding the Functionality that LinkedIn Companies Provides: A Comparison with Facebook Pages

LinkedIn Companies is actually a combination of a number of different modules. In order to better understand how your sales and marketing team can best maximize this multi-functional part of LinkedIn, it's important to understand exactly what the companies functionality offers.

A good way to start is to compare LinkedIn Companies with the most famous corporate presence in social media: The Facebook Fan Page. You could say that a fan page provides details about a company in the "info" section, but this is not the primary way that people are introduced to a company or its page. Rather, the ability for "fans" to "like" a page and then engage with it is what has allowed for the viral spread of information to flow through networks of Facebook friends. The Facebook Page also provides a platform for companies to launch campaigns through the use of custom applications as well as market their products and services through landing pages and other tabs.

Another thing to remember about Facebook Pages is that they were originally called fan pages for a reason: They were organically created by and for fans of popular music, entertainment, and even sports figures. Fan pages were never made for business purposes, and they were never meant to be controlled by a single entity. Over time, as Facebook has concentrated on offering more functionality for businesses that manage pages, it has given administrators more control over those particular pages.

LinkedIn Companies, on the other hand, was created to help both job seekers and professionals conduct research on companies that are represented on LinkedIn.[25] The data was originally pre-populated through a combination of efforts by LinkedIn, user-generated content from LinkedIn profiles, and some statistical information from BusinessWeek.[26] In fact, the ability to search companies was not added until a few months later, and, even then, it was designed as a tool people could use to map out their connections to a particular company. In other words, if you were looking for a business provider with certain expertise, you could see if any of your first-degree connections were employed by such a company. This component of LinkedIn Companies, which is really the purpose of the application, has not changed.

Now that you understand the basic structural and usage differences as well as the histories behind the LinkedIn Companies Page and the Facebook Fan Page, let's move on to a more thorough explanation of the modules available with the current company pages:

- Users can search companies by keyword, location, industry, relationship, company size, number of followers, and Fortune status.
- The overview page for a particular company has information about who connects you to that company, as well as about its employees, Twitter updates, recent blog posts, mentions in the news, and general statistics.
- A statistics page, accessed through the overview page, is completely comprised of user-generated content from profiles and provides employee information for job seekers (such as job function composition, years of work experience, and educational degrees attained by current employees) as well as business intelligence that could be used for sales and business development purposes (such as new employees, former employees, and most recommended employees).

25. http://blog.linkedin.com/2008/03/20/three-two-one-g/
26. http://blog.linkedin.com/2008/03/20/company-profile/

- The careers page within a company's page notes job openings.
- The products and services page is created by the company to showcase its products and services. LinkedIn users can recommend a company's products and services, and their recommendations appear here.
- A "follow company" button allows any LinkedIn user to stay updated on new jobs, hires, and departures from any company's page.
- Administrators of company pages have access to an analytics page as well.

Overall, the LinkedIn Companies module offers a unique hybrid of components, both user-generated and manually populated, that allow your business to have a singular corporate presence on LinkedIn. Optimizing the LinkedIn profile gives your *employees* the opportunity to be found in searches; optimizing your LinkedIn Companies Page increases the chances that your *company* will be found on LinkedIn.

Establishing Your Companies Page

Due to the professional demographic of LinkedIn, it's only a matter of time before more businesses leverage the professional opportunities available by searching for products and services through LinkedIn Companies. It is in every business owner's best interest to ensure that his or her company be found prominently in the search results when someone decides to look for a business that specializes within the company's niche area. To further enhance the experience, the page for your company should be complete, accurate, and enticing for potential customers. Here is what you can do to properly establish your firm in LinkedIn Companies:

1. Take control.

LinkedIn might have already created your page automatically, but now it is time for you to register yourself as the person who edits and controls the page. Assuming that you currently work at the company, you will be able to edit your company's page by changing the settings for the page. The first thing you should do is define who will be the

Companies ▸ Windmill Networking (edit mode)

Overview Careers Services Analytics

This page was last edited on 04/20/2011 by Neal Schaffer

Publish Cancel

• Indicates required field

Company Name: Windmill Networking

❶

Company Pages Admins

◉ All employees with a valid email registered to the company domain

◯ Designated users only

Standard Logo

WindMill NETWORKING.

Edit ❷

Square Logo

Edit

Square logo is used in the network updates

❸

* Company Description

Windmill Networking (DBA Windmill Marketing), founded by social media thought leader Neal Schaffer, is a team of experienced web developers, bloggers & content developers, and social media marketers providing social media strategy consulting services, coaching, training, monitoring, and analytical reporting to B2B and B2C businesses. Windmill Networking has provided social media strategy consulting services to companies that range in size from startup to Fortune 500.

Company Specialties

B2B & B2C social media strategy consulting & coaching	social media & networking speaker
social media training	social media marketing
LinkedIn speaker & workshop	LinkedIn consulting
social media ROI	Internet marketing
Inbound marketing	

⊕ Add more specialties

Twitter ID ❹

nealschaffer

ex: linkedintweets

Company Blog RSS Feed

http://windmillnetworking.com/blog/feed

ex: http://feeds.feedburner.com/blogspot/windmill-networking

News module

When your company is featured in the news.

◉ Show news about my company

◯ Don't show news about my company

*Company Type

Privately Held

*Company Size

2-10

*Company Website URL

http://windmillnetworking.com

*Main Company Industry

Marketing & Advertising

*Company Operating Status

Operating

Year Founded

2009

Company Locations
(Add up to 5 different locations)

❺

Headquarters
1280 Bison Ave., B9-373
Newport Beach, CA 92660
United States

Edit

⊕ Add another location

FIGURE 5.1 *LinkedIn Companies Page Creation*

administrators of this page. LinkedIn allows everyone who has a registered email address with your company's domain to become an automatic administrator, but this should be limited to your key marketing staff who will oversee the page. There is no engagement on a LinkedIn Companies Page like there is on a Facebook Page, so there is really no internal need to have too many administrators for your company's page.

2. Establish your visual branding.

There are two logos that you can upload: One standard logo for the general companies page and a square logo that will appear on the network updates of your followers when your company posts an update. The square logo is critical because it will appear on all of your followers' network updates, so make sure users know at one glance from what company the network updates are coming. Also, make sure that this square logo is accurately shaped; you don't want to distort your logo.

3. Write a keyword-optimized company description and specialties section.

Just as you would embed keywords in your LinkedIn profile so it appears prominently in LinkedIn people searches, you want to do the same with your company's description and specialties. Choose keywords that your potential customers might look for instead of words that simply make your company sound sophisticated, so your company appears in relevant LinkedIn Companies searches. Though you'll need to keep your corporate branding in mind when you complete your company's page, it can help to tweak some of the verbiage so that your company floats to the top during a LinkedIn Companies search. LinkedIn prevents you from overstuffing keywords into the specialties section by enforcing a limit of 20 specialties and 256 cumulative characters.

4. Make your company's page social.

LinkedIn allows you to enter a Twitter handle and your company blog's RSS feed on the company page. Exploit this feature for the potential that every viewer of your page will begin to engage with your company by liking or commenting on your content, which will now be featured on the overview tab of your company's page. This will also give potential customers more context for your company.

5. Location, location, location: take advantage of it.

When professionals search for a service provider, chances are they look for someone close to home, and they can do this by entering their company's ZIP code into the appropriate field when searching for companies. LinkedIn gives you the ability to add up to five different locations for your company, so if you have multiple locations, make sure you utilize this function so that locations in your biggest potential markets are represented for maximum exposure.

Promoting Your Products and Services

Properly establishing your company's page helps people find it in company searches, but it also allows you to showcase your company's branding message and specific specialties. To truly maximize the LinkedIn Companies functionality, however, you are only halfway done with your work here; establishing a products and services page gives LinkedIn users the opportunity to recommend your company, which allows your business to become a trusted company within the professional demographic of LinkedIn.

Some companies, such as Dell, already have nearly 40 products and services listed here.[27] When you add a new product or service, LinkedIn goes into painstaking detail by asking whether it is a product or service and in what category it fits. Right now there is no way of performing searches for these fields of information, but one can only assume that once the LinkedIn database that stores all of the information for companies listed on the site is filled with enough products and services, this will be a searchable option on LinkedIn. It is therefore in every company's best interest to have a complete page as well as a bank of products and services that can be found in a search.

The services tab serves two purposes; it helps potential customers delve into your specific offerings with more detailed information, and also makes

---

27. http://www.linkedin.com/company/dell/products

it easy for past customers to recommend those same services and products. For that same reason, it might make more sense to group your services into a few categories, though you may need to revisit this if LinkedIn creates a products and services search option.

Regardless of how many services you list, LinkedIn makes it easy for you to add a product or service with an 11-step process, which you should follow to make the most of this free marketing opportunity LinkedIn provides. Step 4 and Steps 7 through 11 in particular allow you to flex your promotion muscle:

Step 4: Images make strong statements

LinkedIn is a very text-centric site with profile photos displayed in a relatively small size. This is why those visual ads on the right-hand side of many LinkedIn screens seem to grab our attention. If there is an image to represent your product, it can help items listed on your service page attract potential customers. If your service has no visual, consider using a stock image similar to what you would use on your company's website.

Step 7: Create a custom landing page for your product

The ROI of social media marketing is primarily measured using metrics. You could simply add a Google analytics or other analytical suffix to your product URL to measure leads and conversions from your LinkedIn Companies Page, but I recommend you go one step further. A website visitor who has already gone through the effort of searching for, finding, and delving into your services page and then finally clicking on a link to pursue your product or service is certainly as pre-qualified a social media lead as you will find. In recognition of this, consider creating a custom landing page on your website that appeals to the LinkedIn demographic, which allows you to acknowledge where they came from and offer more targeted information and a customized call to action.

Step 8: Add the right contact people

You have the ability to add three contact people to your company's page. List three people here if at all possible in order to give potential clients a

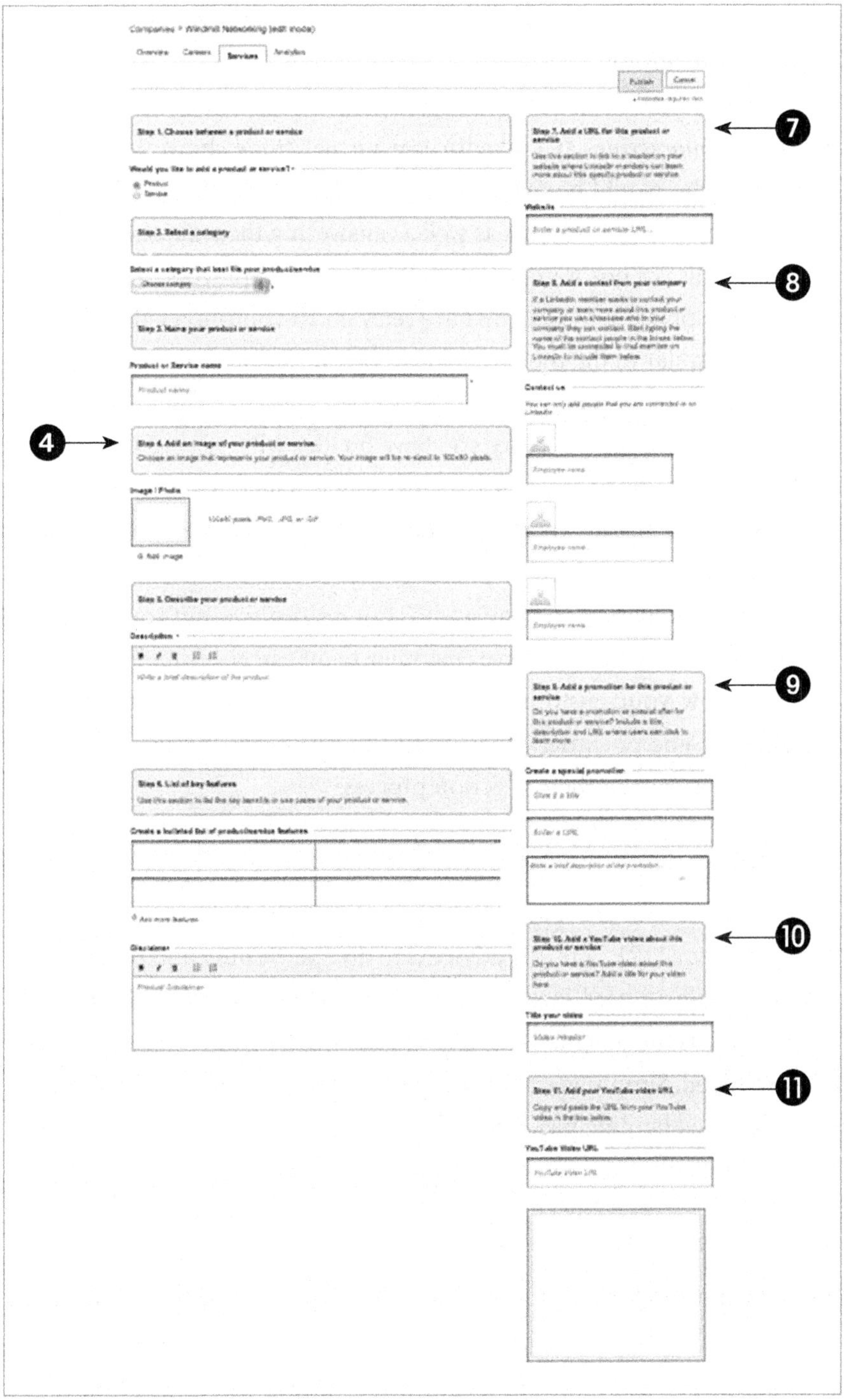

FIGURE 5.2   *LinkedIn Companies Page Services Tab Creation*

choice of contacts. Employees in the following positions may be relevant options for inclusion:

- *Product marketing.* If LinkedIn is a virtual trade show, these are the people who would be manning the booth and offering product information to potential clients as well as answering their questions.
- *Sales.* This is a no-brainer, but it's best to add employees from a variety of geographical locations that are relevant to your targeted customers. This is similar to the thought process behind having multiple locations listed on your overviews tab.
- *Business development.* Since you have no idea what type of client might contact your business, and the prospect might not want to talk to a sales person, having a business development representative listed as a contact might make sense.
- *Customer support.* This may sound counterintuitive, but your customer support representatives have customer management training, and they know how your customers use your products. Before investing in a vendor, some potential clients might prefer to test out your customer support as part of their selection process.

Step 9: Use a promotional URL

LinkedIn gives your company the opportunity to provide a special promotion as well as a URL here. My advice is to do double duty and use the same product URL you used in step seven. If you add promotional language to the page, it has the potential to make prospective customers feel special and acknowledged. Simply add a contact form to the page and you have created a very targeted landing page that will hopefully convert some of the traffic on your LinkedIn Companies Page into measurable future business.

Steps 10 and 11: Add a YouTube video

Video is the most powerful medium that you can use in social media marketing. This is an ideal place to spotlight a video with either customer testimonials or a message from someone knowledgeable about the product; it essentially becomes a virtual demonstration for visitors. Use the video to give just enough information so prospective customers proceed to the promotional URL, and make sure you add the call to action at the end of the video or during the "demonstration" so that your company can increase your chances of capturing the lead.

Reputation Management on LinkedIn Companies

Just as recommendations are the golden currency of LinkedIn profiles because they give the receiver instant credibility, recommendations on LinkedIn Companies Pages can do the same for your company. If many of your company's followers indicate that your company is relevant in your industry by providing recommendations for the products and services you feature on your company's page, this can be the deciding factor in whether you receive new business. While traffic volume to LinkedIn Companies Pages is hard to gauge at this juncture, LinkedIn as a whole received more than 60 million website visits in May 2011.[28] If only one percent of those visitors browsed company pages, that is still 600,000 potential visitors who could be looking at your products and services. Regardless of how many leads actually convert, it doesn't take a significant investment of time to share your products and services with your network of customers, who in turn can generate recommendations.

Even though your company might be marketing your services to other businesses, keep in mind that it is people—not companies—that make the final purchasing decisions. These are the same people who, as online consumers, trust recommendations from people they know 90 percent of the time and even trust recommendations from those they don't know 70 percent of the time.[29] It may be worthwhile to employ an astute marketer within your company to gather recommendations from your customers for your company's page as this can help establish a robust presence on LinkedIn. As more recommendations are made for your company's products and services, more people will find that their network connections are the ones who made those recommendations. This helps

---

28. http://siteanalytics.compete.com/linkedin.com/
29. http://www.bazaarvoice.com/resources/stats

CASE STUDY

Leveraging Customer Loyalty
with a Companies Page

LinkedIn's Companies Pages offer more than just a place to display products and services. Though a bit limited compared to groups, these pages have one important difference; those people who choose to follow a company already have a vested interest in what it does. Harnessing this customer loyalty on a company's page provides them with a place to chime in about what they like about a particular business. As this momentum grows, so does the opportunity for increased business.

BACKGROUND

Rypple[1] is a company that creates social software that helps professionals achieve their goals at work by staying focused, learning faster, and working better together. Because of the nature of the product, employees at Rypple have always focused on building a community of delighted customers on the social networks in which the company is active. These same social networks give customers a voice and platform to share what they really think of a product or service. For this reason, the company has always appreciated the value of LinkedIn and actively uses LinkedIn Groups, Polls, and Ads.

Rypple was invited to be one of the first users of LinkedIn's recently revamped companies pages. Decision makers at the company were particularly excited about LinkedIn Companies Pages for three reasons:

1. It was a new way to engage with others on LinkedIn.
2. It was a trusted way to engage with others while creating a community based around common ideas.
3. It took the concept of LinkedIn Groups in a new direction by providing an easy way for people to come together around a shared interest in Rypple.

---

1. http://rypple.com

WHAT HAPPENED

Those behind the social media efforts at Rypple found it very easy to create the LinkedIn Companies Page. It didn't require any technical knowledge beyond the simple steps outlined in LinkedIn's user interface. Because the company only has one product, one concern they had about the page was whether they should divide the single product up into several types of products or maintain it as a single product. Rypple's representatives decided to be true to the nature of the company and stick with the single listing even though many companies feature several products on their pages.

After Rypple's LinkedIn Companies Page was created, the staff behind it sent out a message to their network that said they were trying out this new LinkedIn feature and the company's connections were welcome to check it out. The point of the message was not to sell the page but simply to engage the company's clients. After sending this message, the company saw a steady increase in the number of recommendations for its product on the page. The decision makers at Rypple are especially happy about the recommendations because:

- There is a photo, name, and kind words attached to each recommendation.
- Compared to a simple "like" on Facebook, it takes more time to leave a recommendation on LinkedIn, which shows the dedication of those who have recommended the product.
- Recommendations are broadcast as network updates by the connections who wrote them.

SUMMARY

The staff at Rypple has been pleasantly surprised with the results of its company's page. Once the product reached 100 recommendations, they noticed that approximately 70 percent of those came from professionals outside of the company's network. They also noticed a tenfold increase in traffic to their company's page compared to before sending out the message. Traffic from LinkedIn to Rypple.com increased by 25 percent. This has led to a 10 percent increase in new user sign-ups coming just from LinkedIn.

solidify your credibility with potential customers who might otherwise be unsure about a purchasing decision. It is also worth noting that product or service recommendations are broadcast to recommenders' networks, and that alone has the potential to spark interest.

Marketers can ask for recommendations from the services page by selecting "request recommendations." Similar to requesting a recommendation for your personal profile, you will need to be connected to those people from whom you want to request a recommendation. This is where tapping into your company's diverse and robust network becomes important. If you are not connected to a particular person from whom you'd like to ask for a recommendation, see if there is someone else within the organization able to facilitate the recommendation request on behalf of your company.

If you represent a small business where a great deal of recommendations from your customers might have already been made to the personal profiles of your founder, president, or executive team members, don't hesitate to contact these previous clients and ask them to resubmit their recommendation for the appropriate product or service on your company's page.

Social Media Marketing and Your LinkedIn Companies Page

Social media does not exist within a vacuum inside your company, and neither should your company's LinkedIn presence. In addition to requesting recommendations for your products and services from your past and present clients on LinkedIn, which helps expose your company and products to your customer's network, there are many ways to use your company's page to integrate your other marketing efforts into this professionally driven network in order to share information about your company and drive targeted leads back to your website. For example:

- Make sure you include your corporate Twitter account and RSS blog feed so social updates flow into the overview tab of your companies page. If you have multiple Twitter accounts for your company, combine the feeds into one account that retweets all of the tweets from your multiple accounts.

- LinkedIn offers a widget that displays a "follow us on LinkedIn" button on your website, which can be found in the bottom right-hand corner of your overview tab. This should be displayed with your other social icons so that interested people can easily follow your company, which, again, enhances credibility and creates a greater opportunity for your blog posts and tweets to spread virally within the LinkedIn community.

- LinkedIn provides a "recommend" button that can be embedded on your website. This displays the current number of recommendations your product has, as well as encourages website visitors to recommend your products and services. The code for this and all other LinkedIn plugins can be found here: http://developer.linkedin.com/community/plugins

- Social ads will be covered in more detail in Chapter 12, but suffice it to say for now that you can create a LinkedIn Ad that drives potential customers straight to the services tab for any given product. While some people say Facebook Ads are more effective because visitors stay within Facebook and don't have to exit the site, at the writing of this book no conclusion can be made regarding the effectiveness of LinkedIn Ads for service tabs because they are so new. If you are using LinkedIn Ads as part of your pay-per-click (PPC) campaign, you might want to experiment with leading potential users to your services tab as well as the LinkedIn landing page for the product on your website.

Engaging Your Company's Followers

As the owner of a LinkedIn Companies Page, you will probably see LinkedIn users start to follow your company. Just as when you follow someone on Twitter, everyone can see everyone else who follows your company. There are many types of people who might be interested in following your company, including job seekers, customers, competitors, and people who would like to do business with you. Considering the fact that your target demographic as a B2B company is on LinkedIn, you should reach out and engage your followers.

Unfortunately, LinkedIn does not offer any tools to help you easily contact your followers. You literally have to look at each profile and contact them one by one, and just because they follow your company does not mean you have extra privileges for contacting them. If you are not connected to these people, and you don't share a LinkedIn Group, you will have to send an InMail to contact them.

Yet that personal engagement is so important. These are professional users who have already expressed an interest in your company just by following you, so it may be advantageous to take the extra step and actually contact them. There are many reasons why you might want to contact your followers from a sales and marketing perspective:

- You want to crowdsource product ideas or get feedback on your services.
- You notice that some of the followers work with your target clients, and they can help you map out the organization and find new business opportunities.
- You are developing business in a new territory or industry and notice that some of your followers work in the sector or area that you are targeting.

As with a lot of sales and marketing in the era of social media, there are no guidelines or set protocols for any of this activity, so strategic outreach must be a result of understanding and using the tools available to us while creatively thinking about new ways to use them in order to lead our companies in new business breakthroughs.

Developing a Targeted Community of Professionals through LinkedIn Groups

---

CHAPTER OBJECTIVES

▪ *Learn about the different kinds of groups on LinkedIn and how each different type of community can be utilized from a sales and marketing or professional networking perspective*

▪ *Learn how to create your own LinkedIn Group and establish industry credibility*

▪ *Explore the functionalities available for managing and monitoring a LinkedIn Group*

▪ *Find strategies to promote and encourage engagement in your group*

ONE OF THE MOST POWERFUL LINKEDIN TOOLS AVAILABLE TO business owners and sales and marketing professionals are the groups. At the time of writing this book there are nearly one million[30] LinkedIn Groups, including those designed for alumni of a certain college or place of employment, corporate groups, groups put together for people attending certain conferences, networking groups serving a specific locale, groups representing associations, and those created for professionals in particular industries. All of these provide the opportunity to grow, develop, and foster established and potentially new business relationships. Because these groups exist on LinkedIn, the demographic is overwhelmingly made up of business professionals aligned with a similar interest or experience.

---

30. http://www.linkedin.com/groupsDirectory?results=

From a corporate sales and marketing perspective, your company is missing out on a plethora of business opportunities if you are not creating and supporting your own community for your target customers on LinkedIn. If your potential customers are interested in talking about a certain subject about which your company has expertise, do you want your company to be the one moderating the conversation, or would you prefer that your customers participated in a conversation led by your competitor? Unlike a Facebook Page, a LinkedIn Group allows you to nurture a community of targeted professionals, influence the dialogue, and, in the end, find a way that is creative and different from LinkedIn's Companies feature to build a fan base of new and potential clients through engaging interaction in your own group. Developing and building this community now will allow you to tap into it for a variety of reasons in the future, such as generating new leads and facilitating introductions that can lead to business development.

From a B2B social media marketing perspective, the way you create a community for professionals in your industry is by seeding the group with conversation and content and sparking engagement. There is no guide for the social web, and professionals are constantly spending more time on the Internet and involved in social media looking for information or recommendations instead of calling up a sales agent or even going to a company website. LinkedIn Groups represents part of this trend, as more and more users are finding affinity with other professionals based around discussions concerning a common topic. If you think about content in this perspective, it's important to decide what information your target demographic is interested in before you ever create a LinkedIn Group. One excellent example of a company that has done this is Philips, which clearly and strategically defined its target demographic before starting the Innovations in Health Group. Though I'll detail this case study more thoroughly later in this chapter, it's worth highlighting this component about who the company is trying to target with its group as stated in its group description:

"Innovations in Health welcomes health professionals interested in sharing, developing and fostering innovative solutions in healthcare. We encourage members to discuss the challenges, opportunities and changes facing our industry. Our goal is to collaborate and share knowledge for progression and seek answers from peers to improve quality and process within health care organizations." [31]

Once you have created your own mission statement that clearly notes your targeted demographic such as the one above, you are ready to create your own LinkedIn Group.

LinkedIn Groups: Virtual Tradeshow Breakout Sessions

LinkedIn Groups are where more and more LinkedIn users are spending their time discussing the latest industry news, creating new relationships, and developing business ideas and deals. According to LinkedIn's latest statistics,[32] there are 17,800,000 members in groups, with 1,500,000 new memberships per week. It is no wonder that there are more than 900,000 LinkedIn Groups, and nearly 20 groups have more than 100,000 members.

Does your industry or profession have an annual tradeshow, conference, or event? If you think attending this particular event has any value, then consider the fact that a LinkedIn Group provides the same facility in an online format that is available 24 hours a day, seven days a week, and is not limited to a single geographic location. You don't have to wait several months for a national event to get industry feedback on your newest product when you can introduce it in your LinkedIn Group to a targeted group of industry professionals who have already shown interest in what your company represents. As an added bonus, groups give you

---

31. http://www.linkedin.com/groups/Innovations-In-Health-2308956
32. http://blog.linkedin.com/100million/

the ability to not only introduce your products and services but also to add value and credibility to your company by establishing and nurturing a community atmosphere that revolves around meaningful conversations and relationships.

From the perspective of a LinkedIn user, if you can't meet someone in person, the next best thing is to foster that coveted relationship online. However, LinkedIn Groups can be a bit overwhelming with so many to choose from and so many different conversations going on at the same time. LinkedIn recently reported that there are an astounding 1,200,000 posts and comments being made to groups every week! With so many options available, you need to create a group that will encourage your target market to join and participate. Therefore, let's take a look at the different types of LinkedIn Groups that exist that might make sense for your company to consider creating. This chapter focuses on the creation and management of LinkedIn Groups for which a marketing division would more than likely be responsible. We go into more detail on the different types of groups that exist and how sales professionals can engage in LinkedIn Groups to develop business in Chapter 7.

Corporate Alumni Groups

Through the natural progress of career growth, most people are likely to work for at least a few different companies throughout their careers. Once people move on, though, they often (and hopefully) continue to hold a natural affinity for their former places of employment.

Because we spend a significant portion of our lives at work, it only makes sense that people become friends with their colleagues, learn from their mentors, aspire to higher positions, and find some sort of pride in having worked at a particular place at some point in time.

As a business owner, you too will have employees come and go, and all of these people can and should be fostered under a group designed for corporate alumni. This is a great place to get people excited about new projects coming down the pipeline—especially because many of your employees had a hand in their creation—and share company successes that can be celebrated by both current and former employees. But work doesn't have to be all work either; don't forget to call out employees who deserve special recognition and also share other lighthearted company news.

If you're wondering why you would want to include former employees in this group, don't forget that, over time, this particular segment of the group will continue to grow as all of these people go on to work for other companies. If you continue to foster the relationships that you built with these members when they were a part of your team, they will likely continue to foster that feeling of belonging and pride of being part of something important. Encourage these people to be part of the extended corporate family and share exciting growth and development news with others. By keeping everyone included in the conversation, you also maintain mindshare with former employees, who might direct other potential employees or customers your way. In fact, your former employees may end up becoming your strongest advocates at their new places of employment.

Industry Groups

Your goal is to position your company as the go-to expert in your particular industry, so why not start a LinkedIn Group that specifically addresses the issues relevant to you and others working in your line of business? By being the company that has established this discussion platform about these industry-specific topics, you immediately establish credibility. By moderating the group, you also have the opportunity to shape the conversations your potential customers and clients are discussing. Provide discussion topics that give you the opportunity to naturally address relevant products, services, and issues for which you want your company known.

In creating your industry-specific group, it's important to make it broad enough so that your potential customers, and not just those working in similar positions at similar companies, feel comfortable with joining and participating in discussions. It's also important to realize that, though you have the opportunity to shape the conversation to a certain extent, you really should allow your group members to express themselves as well. This provides you with valuable insight on what these prospective clients are thinking and how they feel about certain strategies and trends in the marketplace. In many ways, industry-specific groups are like full-time focus groups. Take advantage of the valuable data they have to offer.

Professional Discipline Groups

Industry groups are important for your company to create if you are targeting a specific industry. In addition, some businesses often target specific types of professionals as defined by their discipline or occupation. For instance, if your company offers a technical documentation management software system designed for the aviation industry, you might also want to make your company and its products and services known to technical writers who could potentially become advocates for you within their particular companies.

In many ways, groups that focus on a professional discipline are much broader than industry-specific ones, but both have their benefits, and you might find that it makes sense to create both industry and professional discipline groups. However, realize that since your members in each of these groups might be different, the engagement process will need to be changed appropriately to reflect the different audiences.

Creating Your LinkedIn Community

From a corporate perspective, the ideal way to directly engage with potential customers in the LinkedIn community is to create and lead them into your own group. If your company is large enough, creating an alumni group is something that you should also do, but this chapter focuses on creating a community revolving around an industry. The same advice can be applied if you also want to create a group based on a professional discipline.

Creating a group helps to expand your company's network to professionals with whom you may not have previously interacted, allows you to create a community of potential customers, and provides you with the opportunity to grasp mindshare with interested members.

So how do you create a group? LinkedIn makes it easy for you to do this by selecting "create a group" under the groups menu. From there, all you have to do is fill in the information on one single screen and your group will be created. LinkedIn even conveniently allows you to automatically tweet out the creation of your group if you integrate your Twitter account into your LinkedIn profile.

There's no need to go into great detail on the creation process since it is fairly straightforward, but there are a few areas to note in particular:

Creating Logos

Believe it or not, this is the part of creating a group that could end up requiring the most time. Just as the thumbnail cover of this book may have competed for your attention on Amazon.com, the thumbnail of your logo will compete with all other LinkedIn Groups that pop up when someone searches for a particular keyword. Make sure the image stands out when compared to others; it is also important to brand the group in a way that is attractive to the target audience while maintaining consistency with your established look and feel. When creating the logo you will use for the group, you might want to use the typeface and color that is consistent with your company's branding. To create the best logo possible, you will want to have the logo professionally designed.

Group Name

Your group name is as important as the community you are trying to foster, so think critically about an appropriate group name to best represent your industry. You want to differentiate it from other groups and attract people to your brand, so look at what competing groups are called and create something unique and more appropriate for your specific target demographic. Also, as with the summary of your group, think about what keywords people might use to search for your group and make sure you have keywords in your group name that you want to be associated with. The branding of your group name is important, and you have a lot of real estate to work with here, so maximize the opportunity to ensure maximum discoverability within the LinkedIn Groups search engine.

One thing to note is that on Facebook Pages, companies normally name their page the same as their company or brand name, but you will rarely see this on LinkedIn. Remember that your objective here is to foster a community of current as well as potential customers, not a venue to engage your fans with promotional campaigns. If your group is solely for users of your product then creating a "XX Product Users Group" name makes sense. However, if you're looking to develop new business with your group, in the spirit of inbound marketing, the name of your group should NOT be your company name.

Because LinkedIn is a social networking site, you should choose a name that attracts people and doesn't come off as a sales pitch. For example, if you run a wine company and want to attract restaurant owners and distributors to join your community, consider naming your group something along the lines of "California Wine Fans" or "Wine & Food," which will attract more members while giving you the opportunity to potentially indirectly sell them your wine. Though it makes good business sense to create a page or username that represents your company on Facebook or Twitter, LinkedIn Groups are meant to win the mindshare of your targeted audience and attract them to become members of your group. You can only do so by naming your group appropriately.

Summary

The summary field is meant to spark the interest of anyone who finds your group in a search and wants to learn more. Use this space to briefly summarize your group's missions and goals, but keep SEO in mind when you fill out this area, as a search for groups scans this section. Any keywords that you could not fit into your group name should be listed as part of your summary. At present, the LinkedIn Groups search engine returns keyword results, in descending order of number of group members, for any word that appears in either the title or summary of the group. Make sure you take full advantage of this fact in your summary.

Access

While it might not be necessary to manually approve each requesting member, I suggest that you do so when you first create your group. There are "fake" profiles that exist on LinkedIn; joining groups and planting link-spam disguised as "discussions" is one of the reasons they exist. Though this might not happen at the beginning, the larger your community becomes, the more attractive it becomes for them to join. Furthermore, you can always change and revert back to auto-approve under group settings at any time.

There are two other reasons why it might make sense for you to manually approve each request:

* It gives you the ability to send new members one additional "request-to-join" message using the templates feature that LinkedIn provides (details to follow).
* It allows you to get a feel for how many and what kinds of people are joining your group on a daily basis.

Assuming that you chose "request to join" as the option here, there are four more options that you need to choose. The first two relate to letting your group show up in searches and letting the logo be shown on group members' profiles. You should keep the top two default settings as is so that your group becomes searchable and your logo is visible on the profiles of group members who agree to display it.

The third selection, "Allow members to invite others to join this group," is seemingly innocent; however, if you allow this, any invites that your members send out will not need to be pre-approved. In other words, if you are pre-approving all members, you probably want to close the potential loophole and not enable this function. On the other hand, if you are not pre-approving members, there is no harm in enabling this feature.

The fourth feature here allows you to pre-approve applicants who have email addresses associated with their LinkedIn accounts that use a certain domain (i.e. yourcompany.com would be the domain name for your company). Your group will experience quicker growth and engagement if you give only your employees instant approval and access to your group, but this only works if your employees actually use your company email address for their user profiles. Regardless, you will have the option to manually approve everybody as discussed later in this chapter, so unless you work for a company with thousands or tens of thousands of employees, not

CASE STUDY

Using Groups and Subgroups to Foster Community

It may be tempting to set up a LinkedIn Group specifically to get your company's name out to potentially interested business prospects, but in order to foster a sense of community, you need to let interested constituents communicate with each other about issues that interest them. By leading discussions, answering questions, and otherwise encouraging group members to be active in your group, you help establish credibility for your brand and company in a noninvasive, helpful manner.

BACKGROUND

Though it is historically known for its foray into television, Philips now derives 35 percent of its sales from healthcare and directs much of its B2B marketing toward doctors and hospital staff. Preliminary marketing research on this audience revealed that doctors spend a lot of time on the Internet and appreciate the opportunity to be a part of communities that allow for the sharing of ideas and information. The company also found that more than 5 million medical professionals were already on LinkedIn, and because it wanted to focus on its audience instead of touting its own products, Hans Notenboom, the global director of online CRM for Philips, decided that it only made sense for the company to create its own LinkedIn Group.[1]

WHAT HAPPENED

Philips' objectives for building a community included strengthening its brand, creating promotional opportunities, focusing on clinical staff, building relationships, and facilitating dialogue. In addition to redesigning features on the company website and designing GetInsideHealth.com, the company created the Innovations in Health LinkedIn Group as well as Subgroups specifically for people working in certain areas of medical expertise such as radiology and oncology. Philips

---

1. Case study repurposed with permission from a blog post created by the London-based social media consulting and training company Link Humans (http://linkhumans.com).

fed content into the groups and subgroups from GetInsideHealth.com, and it encouraged interaction with the use of polls, questions, and discussions. Most importantly, however, Philips designed the group so that members could interact with each other about topics pertinent in their professional lives while slowly infusing specific information about the company.

SUMMARY

Innovations in Health now has more than 40,000 members and is one of the five largest health-related LinkedIn Groups. Membership has steadily increased since the group's formation. As stated by Notenboom, "Doctors from India to the U.S. to Germany can now share insights and experience in an environment where we play the facilitator in an unobtrusive way. This is vital for ensuring the conversation stays focused and flows easily, delivering real benefits to our audience."

selecting anything here shouldn't affect the overall efficiency of managing your group.

Open or Members-Only Group

The open LinkedIn Group is a relatively new feature, but unless you don't want your group to be discoverable by others, you'll definitely want to create an open group. Specifically, open groups have the following advantages over members-only groups:

- Discussions are visible to anyone on LinkedIn.
- All discussions are indexed by search engines.
- Discussions can be easily shared on Twitter and Facebook.

From a marketing perspective, open groups win hands down. That said, if you create an alumni-only group or perhaps a group that would include only actual users of your products that you want to exercise tight control over, you would want to create a members-only group and restrict conversations behind a firewall of privacy.

Establishing LinkedIn Group Settings and Policies

Once you create your group and before you begin promoting it, set it up for success by navigating through the various settings and establishing membership policies for your group. If you've ever been an administrator for a Facebook Page you will be pleasantly surprised, and perhaps confused, by the various options that LinkedIn offers to help with group moderation. This diverse selection of tools really is on the cutting edge of online community management.

You can find all of the group management tools under the "manage" tab, which will then display a host of options in the "manage group" menu on the left-hand side of the screen. The following settings are the ones you should concentrate on in order to manage the infrastructure of your group. These are located in the fourth out of five sections in this menu, beginning with "group settings" and ending with "subgroups."

Group Settings

The settings you can modify here include forum tabs you can enable, permissions, restrictions, and modifications to the original membership rules of auto-join vs. request to join. Let's look at some of these settings in more detail:

FORUM TABS

By default, the discussion and news features are enabled, as this is where your community will primarily be engaging. Beyond that, you have the ability to enable promotions and jobs features. Enabling these will create new "tabs" in the menu from which your members can select. Furthermore, there is the option to allow only managers and moderators to move discussions to promotions and jobs tabs as well as the ability to automatically remove some of these postings if a certain number of members flag them as spam.

These options exist because some LinkedIn Groups have a history of spam accumulation. This is due to the lucrative demographic of the LinkedIn user as well as the sheer number of users who are active on some groups. Enabling the promotions and jobs tabs gives you the ability to

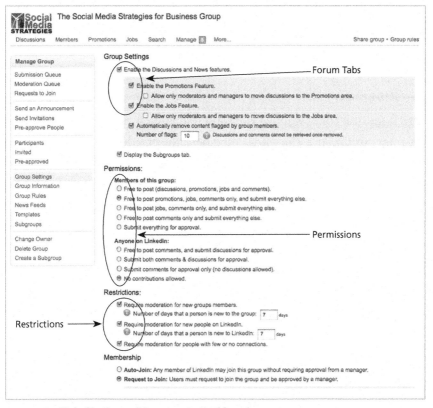

FIGURE 6.1 LinkedIn Groups Management Dashboard

move discussions that aren't really relevant to the group mission—such as someone promoting their latest webinar or an announcement of a new job opening—to a completely separate tab. Allowing anyone in the group to moderate as well as flag inappropriate content allows for an element of crowdsourcing wherein your group members help moderate your group.

Until your group gets a few thousand members, it will be easy for you to moderate it without spending much time, so you may choose not to enable the promotions and jobs features if you want to concentrate on discussions. Furthermore, since you will be directly moderating your group, there is no need to automatically remove content that is flagged. On the other hand, if you would rather have a loosely moderated group and believe you can grow your community faster by allowing all of your members to promote their services and post jobs, you may want to enable these features. Regardless of the strategy you choose, you have the ability to delete any post that goes against the group policies you create, which will be discussed later in this chapter.

PERMISSIONS

This is the heart of how much you want to manually moderate submissions for your group. You can allow members the freedom to post anything without moderation, or you can require that everything be submitted for approval. If you want to moderate discussions that are posted, which I recommend you do, you'll want to select one of the five options under the "members of this group" menu. However, I recommend that you allow members to submit comments on discussions without your approval. Similar to comment moderation on blogs, one of the most potentially damaging things you can do to discourage engagement in your group is not allow comments made by group members to automatically appear when they are made.

If your group is an open one, you will see additional options under "anyone on LinkedIn." Since your group is open, anyone on LinkedIn can view any discussion. However, because you are trying to build a community, you probably only want contributions and comments from actual group members, so choose "no contributions allowed." This encourages those who want to participate in a discussion to actually join your group.

RESTRICTIONS

You should select all three features here to take advantage of the ability to limit your group's exposure to potential spam from new LinkedIn and/or group members as well as those with few connections who want to join your group in order to promote their own products and services. These options mean that new users and/or group members must be subjected to moderation for a certain number of days, so they are still allowed to participate, but selecting these options gives you greater control to ensure community policies are enforced before posts are published that potentially go against your community's spirit.

Group Rules

If you have ever been a member of a LinkedIn Group, you know that many are filled with spammy, link-building "discussions" that tarnish the atmosphere of not only the group but also potentially the brand of the company sponsoring it. Social media marketing is about relevance, so it is important to maintain your group's legitimacy by actively managing it and keeping irrelevant information out. In addition to the settings described above, you should create a LinkedIn Group policy so your members know what the group's purpose is and what types of postings and behavior will not be tolerated and may result in deleted content and even removal from the group.

LinkedIn gives group managers the ability to create and document a group policy under this setting. This is where you can set your expectations and rules for the group so there are no misunderstandings with members should you need to delete spammy posts. Establishing a group policy also highlights your company's professionalism in managing the group, so I recommend taking an extra step and customizing the template LinkedIn provides for welcoming new members (discussed below) and either list the rules or remind members to read them in another location.

Below is an example of the group rules that I posted for my group, The Social Media Strategies for Business:[33]

Welcome to The Social Media Strategies for Business Group!

As the name implies, we are all here to discuss, learn, and share information about social media for businesses. This is not a community for self-promotion, yet you are certainly welcome to share your ideas that you express through your blog posts and for-free webinars so long as they are resourceful and on-topic for the group. Please feel free to start discussions based on interesting blog posts that you find.

---

33. http://wind.mn/windsm

With this in mind, the general rule for the group is WE WILL NOT TOLERATE SPAM. Spam is defined as subject matter that is not related to the group mission detailed above. Any post that is not relevant to social media strategies for business will be deleted and the contributor blocked from this group. If you are in doubt, ask me, Neal Schaffer the Group Manager, by LinkedIn Message or email (nealschaffer@gmail. com) BEFORE you post. I will try to respond within 24 hours.

Thank you, and I am sincerely looking forward to both your contributions and in making this a LinkedIn Group where intellectual discussion on social media strategy flourishes. And if you have any questions, comments, or concerns about this group at any time, do not hesitate to reach out and contact me.

Neal Schaffer
http://windmillnetworking.com

News Feeds

LinkedIn gives you the ability to add a news feed utilizing RSS technology so that your company blog posts are automatically posted as a discussion. I tell all of my social media strategy consulting clients to avoid the temptation to automate. You spent time crafting your content, so spend another minute to add a personalized touch by introducing the content to your group members. In other words, you probably won't need—or want—to use this feature, however convenient it might seem.

Templates

LinkedIn gives you the ability to send an automated message that you create under any or all of the following conditions:

- Someone requests to join your group (and you have chosen to manually approve each person).
- Someone joins your group and you want to send a welcome message.
- You want to decline someone membership in your group.

- You want to decline and block someone from joining your group again.

At a minimum, I suggest you create a message to welcome new members and give them a brief tutorial of the group. This also gives you the ability to highlight what you expect from new members, point out your group rules, and add a bit of information about your company to start building corporate mindshare as well. While asking new members to join a mailing list might be a little aggressive for some, here is a sample of my own welcome message template for you to consider while drafting your own:

Thank you for joining The Social Media Strategies for Business Group!

Group rules have been established for this community, so please make sure you read them before participating. They appear at the top right-hand corner of any screen in this group.

Please read the discussions boards and feel free to start discussions or submit news that can better help businesses understand social media strategies. The more members we have, the more news submitted and discussions to engage in, the more value this group will have for everyone. Please encourage your friends to also join by sending them this link:

http://www.linkedin.com/groups?&gid=2321400

Also, since you joined this group, I encourage you to sign up for my email newsletter which gives you the latest information on lots of other social media resources that I am confident you'll be interested in. I send out the newsletter at most once a month, and as a thank you for joining I am giving away a few free chapters from my "Windmill Networking: Understanding, Leveraging & Maximizing LinkedIn" book.

To join, please visit: http://eepurl.com/c529

Let me know if there is anything that I can do to help you or your business out as well as any feedback that you might have in order to improve our group.

Best regards,
Neal Schaffer
President, Windmills Marketing, a Social Media Strategic Consultancy
Telephone: (888) 541-3429
http://windmillnetworking.com

Moderating Your Group for Success

It goes without saying that effective moderation is imperative to the success of your group and can result in continued growth as more people join, participate, and find value in being a member. Now that you've established the infrastructure for your group according to the preceding information, let's look at the three areas where you will be managing your community on a day-to-day basis: The submission queue, the moderation queue, and requests to join. All three areas are accessible in the first of five sections on the "manage group" menu.

Although it is recommended that you check in on your group on a daily basis as part of your daily LinkedIn routine that I recommend in Chapter 14, you can see if there is any new content in the submission queue or requests to join by simply visiting "your groups" under the "groups" menu and seeing if there are colored shapes with numbers inside them. For instance, anything in the submission queue will be represented by a light orange rectangle while requests to join are indicated by a green circle. These are only visible to managers of your group. The other way you'll know if you need to moderate something is that when you visit your group, a colored shape with a number inside it just to the right of the "manage" tab will indicate the thing that needs attention.

Submission Queue

Depending on your group settings, content that needs to be submitted before approval will appear here. You have the option to approve, move to promotions or jobs (if you have these enabled), or delete each submission. Furthermore, you have the ability to change permissions for each person submitting a discussion or comment by selecting the submission and navigating to the "change permission" box on the top right-hand side above the submission queue. This feature allows you to give specific individuals the right to post or moderate, which will overwrite your general group settings. The option also exists to block and delete specific members from your group. If there are trusted group members, giving them the ability to automatically post will help keep them better engaged with your group. It should be noted that these settings on a per-member basis can also be managed by clicking on "participants" in the "manage group" menu.

Moderation Queue

Similar to the submission queue, the moderation queue is where posts and comments flagged by other members will appear. The same options are available for you as in the submission queue. Until your group achieves a certain mass, you might not see much activity here.

Requests to Join

If you elect to manually approve members when you set up the access setting, this is where you approve all of the requests to join. The options here are to approve, decline, decline and block, or send a message to the applicant. LinkedIn conveniently warns you if the user trying to join your group has few or no connections, a sure sign that they might be joining your group for the wrong reasons.

LinkedIn Group Engagement Strategy

The ultimate goal in establishing a LinkedIn Group is to get people interested in the content and participating in thought-provoking discussions. Just as engaging with fans on your Facebook Page will help draw attention to your news as it is posted to each member's personal news feed, engagement by your LinkedIn Group members will help others find and hopefully join your group when they look at the network updates of their connections.

The challenge is, of course, how to foster that engagement. When starting a LinkedIn Group, group managers need to assume leadership by proactively starting conversations, posting relevant and timely news that interests members, and quickly reacting to the discussions and questions of others. This can be done in a time-effective manner by pre-scheduling your activities with the use of an editorial calendar as well as utilizing LinkedIn's feature that allows group managers to receive updates of new discussions and comments the moment they are made. As membership grows, chances are the discussions will become mostly self-generated, but it's still important to check in on a regular basis and generate new discussions as needed.

Regarding the types of discussions to generate, there really is no one-size-fits-all approach. One tactic used by some group managers is to find an interesting discussion taking place in another group and either repurpose it for your specific group's focus or, if it is a discussion with unique content, give credit to the person who started the discussion in the other group. Posing open-ended questions is a particularly good way to get people talking, especially when your group is new. Another popular type of discussion, especially when you first start the group, is the "introduce yourself" post.

It's one thing to create a group, but what do you after you've started discussions and membership begins to grow? Every person's objective for creating a group will be different, but the common thread among all groups is that you must communicate well with your members and provide them with value so that they stick with it. There are always new groups being created that will compete with your group for membership because of LinkedIn's current 50-group maximum for members.

Your options for communicating and providing value to your group to make it a cohesive and valuable one really come down to generating new discussions and monitoring the current ones. After all, creating, participating in, and fostering discussions is how you will generate activity and interaction. If you have an interesting topic to discuss, actively start a discussion about it. Because group members may receive weekly digests of group activity, it is important to do this at least once a week if possible so there is always fresh content going out to your members. Make the discussion interesting, ensure that it provides value, and try to generate lively conversation. Don't forget to comment on everyone else's discussions, which may encourage them to contribute more.

In addition to the above, here are a few other engagement vehicles that LinkedIn provides to foster greater participation:

Top Influencers This Week

A widget appears on the right-hand side of all of your group pages indicating the top influencers of your group. While the algorithm for calculating this is not public, it is no mystery that those who contribute posts that are heavily liked or commented on will be displayed here. To foster further engagement, encourage your top influencers to contribute more, and check in with a comment on their discussions regularly.

Manager's Choice

A group manager has the ability to select any given discussion to become the "manager's choice," a distinction that appears prominently at the top right-hand corner of the landing page for your group. The person who started the conversation will have their photo prominently displayed in this space, so think of this selection as another way of thanking and encouraging further engagement from those group members whose participation you value.

The "Like" Button

Are there discussions that you particularly like? Suggest that others check out the conversation and encourage the contributor to submit more by clicking on the thumbs-up icon. Simply "liking" a discussion gives it your seal of approval and provides the discussion with more visibility in your group as well as your network updates.

The "Announcement" Feature

The final engagement vehicle, the announcement feature, will be discussed in more detail later in this chapter as a call-to-action vehicle. Use it as a means to further engagement, however, by highlighting a discussion that is generating a lot of comments or calling out a new discussion in which you would like everyone to participate.

Finding Relevant Content to Share in Your New Group

The challenge of managing your LinkedIn Group will be to keep the discussions lively and the content fresh. What types of discussions and content would be most interesting to your community members? Your ability to find sources of relevant content to share in your new group when discussions are lagging is a critical one to meet your group's needs.

There are many potential places to look for material, but it is important for you to find the right sources of content that will be relevant to your audience. Compile a list of at least ten sources of content and, if possible, subscribe to their RSS feeds using an RSS reader (such as Google Reader)[34] so you can monitor content that might be of interest to your group members. Here are some potential sources of content to consider:

- Your company blog
- Relevant industry or professional association website news and blog posts
- Popular industry news from LinkedIn Today ("news" on LinkedIn's top menu)
- Create a Google Alert[35] for a relevant keyword
- Search on Twitter or use Twitter search engines such as Topsy[36] for popular conversations revolving around your keywords

The Announcement Feature: Your Call to Action

Using an announcement is the only way to communicate with all of your group members at once, assuming they have enabled the default

---

34. http://*www.google.com/reader*
35. http://*www.google.com/alerts*
36. http://topsy.com

setting when they joined your group. You can select this feature through the "manage group" menu under "send an announcement." Because the announcement will go straight into your members' inbox, you don't want to overuse this feature and potentially be seen as a spammer—giving your members a good reason to leave your group. For this reason, LinkedIn limits you to only one announcement per week.

You can also choose to make an announcement a featured discussion to appear as the manager's choice. By doing so, you ensure that those who are not receiving announcements still have a chance to read the information you want to disseminate.

The announcement feature is best utilized when there is a strategic "event" that would be extremely relevant and timely to present to your targeted audience. For instance, if you will be exhibiting at a (physical) industry trade show and are able to provide a discount code to attendees, your users would likely find value in that message. Perhaps you are offering a free webinar or have a resourceful white paper that you are giving away. This may be something you want to announce as well. There is no single rule regarding how often announcements should be sent and what content should be included in them, but proper utilization of this feature can help your business maintain mindshare and strengthen your brand awareness on LinkedIn.

One way to think about announcements is that they are similar to sending newsletters to your email subscribers. You want to ensure that the content is useful to them so they will open it, and there is nothing wrong with including your call to action as part of the content. However, sending the newsletter too often may make people unsubscribe. On the other hand, if you don't send out the newsletter often enough, your subscribers may forget about you. Use this as a guideline for the timing and content of your announcements.

Promoting Your LinkedIn Group

We've gotten a little ahead of ourselves here, because there can be no engagement or moderation without any group members. In fact, after you put the finishing touches on your group and triumphantly make it public, it can be a bit disappointing to see that it only has one member…you. Regardless of whether you're starting a group from scratch or you've had one up and running for awhile, you need to promote what it has to offer in order to ensure its growth and success.

Promotion for any group usually starts with your own company's network of connections. If you want to send out invitations to encourage people to join your group, LinkedIn distributes emails on your behalf by selecting the "invite others" option under "share group," which appears next to your group rules on the top right-hand corner of your group's page. By pressing the "in" logo that appears at the far right of where you enter your connections, you can easily navigate through your own connections by industry and location and send out 50 invitations at a time. Sending out invitations using the official LinkedIn functionality is efficient in that it allows recipients of the invitation to easily join your group from the message. Just as with any other communication tools on LinkedIn, make sure you personalize your message so it provides an incentive for potential members.

It also goes without saying that you should only send group invitations to those you think might be interested in joining. Many LinkedIn users are annoyed when they receive invitations for groups that are totally irrelevant to them, and it's because of the prevalence of blanket invitations that many people view some groups as spam.

In your group introduction, include details regarding the group and your brand messages that will resonate with your targeted demographic. It is important to differentiate yourself from the hundreds of thousands of LinkedIn Groups that already exist. Potential members should find value in joining your group, so provide a good reason for those reading the invitation to become members. In essence, if you think about your target audience, integrate branding and differentiation in your message, and outline the benefits of joining your LinkedIn Group, you stand a much higher chance of success when emailing prospective members.

You will be at an advantage for promotion if many of your employees are already established users with LinkedIn connections. Of course, just as you would target your message, your employees should also only introduce your group to those who are in your target demographic and would find it a valuable resource.

If you choose to create a group that focuses on a particular demographic or industry, try to connect with the power connectors in that demographic; they can be found by doing a targeted advanced people search, which displays results sorted by number of connections. Let them know about your group, and, if they join, others that look at their profiles may find your group and join as well. If you followed my advice on strategically expanding your network in Chapter 4, you should already be connected with these "super connectors."

You might also find value in visiting the discussion boards in similar groups in which you are a member and posting a message introducing the new group. It is obviously in your best interest to look at the group rules and contact the group manager first to see if he or she is comfortable with your doing so. As long as you differentiate your group as being complementary to the group on which you would like to post, and you agree to post your message once and then move on, you just might be approved to do so. Offering them a chance of jointly promoting their group to your community is recommended for this type of approach.

Promotion doesn't and shouldn't stop with LinkedIn members: Once you begin to strategically engage in social media, you need to optimize your own website to embrace that strategy. For a LinkedIn Group, this outreach can be as simple as posting a logo with a clickable link in a prominent location on your website that leads to your group. This allows visitors to your website to learn about your community and easily join it. If you publish an email newsletter, make sure you feature your LinkedIn Group logo there as well. An occasional tweet or Facebook post introducing your LinkedIn Group is another way to efficiently utilize social media to advertise and promote your LinkedIn Group.

Finally, LinkedIn provides two different ways to easily share your open group on Twitter, Facebook, and LinkedIn that you should utilize. The first is to use the "share group" functionality that you may have used to invite other LinkedIn members to join. Above that selection, LinkedIn

CASE STUDY

Creating a LinkedIn Group to Promote Interest in an Event

If you are organizing a conference, workshop, or other relevant event for industry professionals, consider letting your connections on LinkedIn know, and be creative when reaching out to others who might be interested. Many people working in sales, marketing, and business development are constantly looking for new educational opportunities to improve their skills and network with other industry professionals in person.

BACKGROUND

Lanette Hanson, a business professional with more than eight years of experience in organizing workers' compensation and risk management educational programs, started her own educational firm in 2010. As an entrepreneur on a tight marketing budget, she turned to LinkedIn to build awareness of the California Workers' Compensation & Risk Conference,[1] a new program she is producing, as well as identify hot topics and secure industry expert speakers.

WHAT HAPPENED

Though it was potentially a bit risky, Hanson created a LinkedIn Group called California Workers' Compensation & Risk Conference, the same name as the event she was producing. When she invited others to join the group, she promoted the fact that the group was designed for educational purposes and discussion on industry topics so as not to turn off anyone who might not be interested in the conference itself. In the group, Hanson used the discussion feature to encourage conversation on the industry's most pressing issues, and she also posted event information on a weekly basis. In addition, Hanson posted conference information in her other groups and in her status updates.

SUMMARY

Within four months of actively using LinkedIn to promote her conference, Hanson was able to track that 60 percent of her attendee

---

1. http://www.cwcriskconference.org

registrations were through the site due to a discount code she published with all of her posts. In other words, her LinkedIn efforts, which spawned from the creation of a LinkedIn Group, resulted in 60 percent of her firm's yearly revenue.

conveniently provides a shortcut to share the group on your LinkedIn Status Update as well as on Twitter and Facebook. Not only should you do this after creating your group, but also consider doing this at regular monthly, bimonthly, or quarterly intervals to remind your ever growing network of the group's presence.

You can also utilize the "share this discussion" feature to promote your group via social media. This is found at the top left-hand side of every discussion in an open group. By enticing your LinkedIn connections, Facebook friends, and Twitter followers with a popular discussion or content from your group, you can lead them to your group where the value is laid out for them and joining is a simple click away.

Subgroup Strategies: Is It Time to Create One?

You'll notice that I haven't talked about subgroups until now, and that's for good reason: If you are trying to build a community, you need to first establish yourself before branching out and trying to establish several communities at once. Once your group reaches a certain point, however, it might make logical sense to further break down your community by creating subgroups for the following types of group member classification:

* Geography
* Industry or sub-industry
* Product line
* Profession

There is another reason why you might want to create a subgroup, and that is the SEO benefit of having any one of your communities found when someone is performing a LinkedIn Group search. For instance, let's say there are dozens of keywords associated with your industry for which you created your group. You could create subgroups for each subset of keywords that you weren't able to include in the description text of your main group. This can be extremely effective for subgroups based on geography, for instance, because if there are key markets that your company is targeting, you could include those geographical names as part of the group name or description. In this way, subgroups can significantly boost the discoverability of your community within the LinkedIn Group search engine.

The same logic about discoverability can also help boost membership in the parent group, which is what LinkedIn refers to as the original group, when you create subgroups that fall beneath it. This is because, should a LinkedIn user find your subgroup and want to join it, they will automatically have to simultaneously submit an application to join your parent group.[37] Thus, when people discover and choose to join a subgroup, it automatically gives you the opportunity to foster a larger parent group community.

You'll go through the same process to create a subgroup as you did when creating your original group. You can create a new subgroup by selecting the "manage" tab in your group and clicking on "create a subgroup" from the "manage groups" menu on the left-hand side. Though the selections for subgroups are the exactly the same as for groups, there is one option missing: At the time of writing this book, subgroups can only be created as members-only groups, not open groups. Furthermore, it should be noted that a maximum of 20 subgroups can be created for each parent group.[38]

As with social media in general, the more accounts or communities you own, the more time it will take to promote as well as generate valuable engagement. Though you could create subgroups simply for discoverability purposes, members might not stick around long enough if there is little or no engagement. My recommendation is that you consider experimenting with subgroups only when you've reached a certain mass. This number will differ from group to group, but I wouldn't even consider creating one until you have close to 1,000 members.

---

37. http://wind.mn/lianswers1
38. http://wind.mn/lianswers2

7

The Many Ways
to Engage on LinkedIn

CHAPTER OBJECTIVES

■ *Provide strategies for maximizing engagement opportunities in LinkedIn Groups*

■ *Understand how to use LinkedIn Answers to find new business*

■ *Learn how to use network updates, events, and other LinkedIn applications to engage with other users for professional networking and business development*

WHILE THERE ARE MANY WHO THINK THAT ENGAGEMENT only happens in social media on hyper-social platforms like Facebook and Twitter, there are many ways to engage with potential clients on LinkedIn in order to develop business. In sourcing case studies to showcase how others developed business on LinkedIn, by far the most responses came from engaging in two of the most important forums on LinkedIn: LinkedIn Groups and LinkedIn Answers.

Though the majority of this chapter focuses on using groups and answers as engagement platforms for business development, it is important to know that there are other avenues available for engagement on LinkedIn, which we'll examine at the end of this chapter. With a little out-of-the-box thinking, you will see that there are a variety of areas within LinkedIn where engagement with other users is possible—and business is waiting to be developed.

Groups

Since virtually every profession and discipline is represented at this never-ending, online trade show known as LinkedIn, there is a need to offer separate sessions and space so those with similar interests can converge for discussions and share news on topics of interest. LinkedIn Groups represent these communities of professionals aligned with similar interests, and thus it goes without saying that any sales, marketing, and business development executive needs to be present and "working" the virtual rooms where his or her targeted customers might be. The power of LinkedIn Groups cannot be underestimated; other than the huge public chat room of more than 200 million users that constitutes Twitter, LinkedIn Groups are probably the second largest public forums where B2B decision makers and other professionals are found.

LinkedIn members join groups in order to meet and network with people who have similar professional and educational interests. These groups, then, become in essence a virtual trade show as the hundreds, thousands, or even tens of thousands of members discuss relevant topics, post questions, seek out business opportunities, and promote the services and products they represent in which other group members would have an interest. LinkedIn Groups are composed primarily of professionals, are concentrated on niche industries or in niche locations (or a combination of the two), and are communities where people regularly participate in the discussions—or at least receive a daily or weekly digest of activities. If you are a business owner or work in sales and marketing, this means LinkedIn Groups provide even more benefit because they can result in more business.

The Advantages of Group Engagement

Functionality provided by LinkedIn Groups is surprisingly simple: All you have is a discussions board and a membership list, both of which are completely searchable. There might be a promotions or jobs tab enabled, but from the business perspective, these are not areas where you'll spend much time. Though the functionality of LinkedIn Groups appears to be quite simple, it offers an impressive array of ways for business professionals to engage with others and develop business, including the following:

MESSAGING

LinkedIn Groups allow you to be virtually connected to a number of people that share a common interest with you. This is accomplished not merely by joining the group, but also through the functionality that allows members to send each other messages without being directly connected as long as they're in the same group.

To put this in perspective, consider the following: One of the largest LinkedIn Groups, eMarketing Association Network,[39] has more than 325,000 members as of June 2011. According to the group description, the community is "Open to all professionals interested in Internet Marketing." If you join this group, you can directly send a message—regardless of connectivity status and without knowing an email address—to any one of the 325,000+ group members. It is important to note that you can directly send a message to a group member who is not directly connected to you only if the person has chosen to receive messages from other group members (which is the default setting).

APPROACHABILITY

Just as you gain the ability to message many others, joining an especially large group like eMarketing Association Network gives potentially hundreds of thousands of people the opportunity to contact you should they have a reason to reach out to you. Thus, mere membership in groups provides potential customers with an easy way to contact you. The ability to see and be seen, especially in your core areas of expertise or interest, gives the added advantage of visibility above and beyond approachability.

---

39. http://www.linkedin.com/groups?gid=41352

CONNECTING

Sales and marketing professionals who hope to open their network beyond their first-degree connections must be involved with groups as it really is the way to meet others beyond those you already know. Participating in discussions and actively engaging in conversations with other group members is one of the best ways to network within the LinkedIn platform. When you "meet" someone in a discussion with whom you think you might want to do business, ask him or her if they would be interested in connecting on LinkedIn. When you send an invitation to connect, simply choose "groups" and then the group you are both a member of from the drop-down menu.

CONVERSATION MONITORING

One of the great features that LinkedIn provides when you sign up for a group is the ability to receive a daily or weekly digest of what is going on in the group. This means that, from the comfort of your inbox and by investing a few minutes of your time, you can quickly scan for only those conversations that may hint at business prospects for you. Consider this; businesses pay a great deal of money for social media monitoring software to monitor online conversations, but this doesn't catch members-only LinkedIn Groups because of their private nature. Furthermore, Twitter and Facebook don't provide functionality to have Facebook Fan Page conversation or @ mentions sent to your email. LinkedIn conveniently provides this to you for free, so take advantage of it and work it into your daily LinkedIn routine, which is covered in Chapter 14.

BE WHERE YOUR CUSTOMERS ARE

Just as your business needs to have a presence in relevant social media channels, you need to be where your potential customers are. If you find the groups your potential customers might be in and join them, you've placed yourself in a situation to actively engage and participate in conversation with them.

Now that you're (hopefully) sold on the importance of joining and participating in LinkedIn Groups, it's time to ensure that you are maximizing your LinkedIn presence by joining the maximum number of groups that LinkedIn permits you to join.

LinkedIn has capped the number of groups a person may be a part of at 50. My recommendation, then, is that you take full advantage of this allowance and join 50 groups. There are nearly one million LinkedIn Groups out there so it shouldn't be hard to find 50 that will help you achieve your sales and marketing objectives. Just put a keyword in the search box for groups and chances are you'll find at least one (and likely more) relevant LinkedIn Groups.

To maximize your presence in groups, I recommend you do not focus all of your effort on one thing and, instead, diversify your membership into a combination of the following types of groups. Each different type offers ways to help you broaden your reach in both contacting and connecting with others and can help you be found by those who are looking for your company's expertise.

Once you've joined a few LinkedIn Groups, you might consider looking through the "groups you may like" option, which can be found under the groups tab. Based on what you've already joined, LinkedIn does a surprisingly good job of compiling other groups that you might find relevant but somehow missed during your keyword searches.

LARGE GROUPS

One day I noticed that, when I didn't enter any text while searching through groups, it returned, in descending order, the LinkedIn Groups with the most members. Since joining a LinkedIn Group allows you to be visible within that Group and also gives you the opportunity to send direct messages to other members, joining a few large groups that are relevant to your objective makes sense. Consider joining the following five groups, each of which have more than 100,000 members currently and are consistently among the most popular groups that are relevant to most sales and marketing professionals:

- eMarketing Association Network[40]—Consistently the largest marketing group

---

40. http://www.linkedin.com/groups?gid=41352

- Executive Suite[41]—Consistently the largest group for executives
- Social Media Marketing[42]—Consistently the largest social media marketing group
- Innovative Marketing, PR, Sales, Word-of-Mouth & Buzz Innovators[43]— Consistently the largest general sales and marketing community
- TopLinked.com[44]—Consistently the largest open networking[45] group

LOCAL GROUPS

There are a plethora of groups that have been created specifically for the purpose of connecting professionals living, working, or wanting to connect with people in a certain geographical region. You should join the following local groups: Communities for where you live, where you work, and also for every major geographic region where your target customers are primarily located. These types of groups can increase your chances of connecting with and being found by those who seek out your company's expertise locally. They also increase your chance of being able to find people with whom to network who might help you connect with an organization you are targeting in a specific geographic area. Regional groups not only allow you to connect with other people interested in a particular geographic area, but they may also alert you of potential face-to-face networking events in that locale. Take advantage of the added benefit of networking face-to-face. Though virtual networking can do wonders for sales and marketing professionals, nothing is as powerful as an honest handshake and actual person-to-person interaction.

ALUMNI GROUPS

There are many groups that specialize in creating LinkedIn communities for alumni of colleges and companies. In addition to directly connecting

---

41. http://www.linkedin.com/groups?gid=1426
42. http://www.linkedin.com/groups/Social-Media-Marketing-66325
43. http://www.linkedin.com/groups/Innovative-Marketing-PR-Sales-WordofMouth-54066
44. http://www.linkedin.com/groups?gid=42031
45. Please read *Windmill Networking: Maximizing LinkedIn* for a detailed introduction to open networking.

to former colleagues, you can join this type of group to find alumni with whom you don't want to directly connect. It simply facilitates more efficient networking with other alumni if you are in the same group.

As students in college (and even high school), most of us weren't thinking about how our classmates, research partners, fraternity brothers and sisters, fellow club members, and friends could assist in our professional goals—after all, we were all just worried about whether we could make it through finals. But there was a point when we all finally graduated and moved on to new and different professional endeavors, and it was at that point that those hundreds of people we met in college had the potential to become valuable connections in our networks. By keeping in touch and fostering the relationships we have with our former classmates, we have the ability to tap into industries in which we wouldn't normally do business and therefore connect with second- and third-degree connections that provide an even further reach into the LinkedIn database. You never know where that party animal from your freshman dorm ended up; he or she may currently be the CEO of the company to which you want to sell your product or service.

One of the advantages of joining an alumni group is that you've likely met many of these people in person, so you instantly have built-in credibility. It can be a bit awkward asking someone you don't know for an introduction or favor on LinkedIn, but joining an alumni group ensures that you will immediately have common ground with anyone you engage in conversation. This will become a cornerstone of your professional networking activities on LinkedIn.

INDUSTRY GROUPS

You need to be a member of the largest Industry groups with which your company is affiliated because this is where you'll meet all of those people at the virtual industry trade show. It is in these groups where you'll learn about the latest industry news and trends, network with other industry professionals, and explore partnerships and alliances with other industry-affiliated companies.

TARGET MARKET GROUPS

Your customers might not necessarily be in the same industry you are, so if this is the case, you need to ensure that you are not only a member of industry groups but also a member of groups where your potential customers are present. You might not be able to join some of these groups if you do not have the same professional background or currently work in the same industry they do, but be creative in your group searches and you are bound to find some groups specific to your target market where you will be welcomed as a member. Remember, LinkedIn doesn't dictate who gets accepted into individual groups. That responsibility falls on the group manager, whom you can always contact if you feel that you have been unfairly rejected from the group.

LinkedIn Group Engagement Strategy

The engagement process in LinkedIn Groups is actually quite simple; join a group and check the discussions to see how relevant they may or may not be to your business. Participate in a discussion, or better yet, try starting one of your own to gauge interest. Post a link to an interesting blog post you read that you think might spark conversation. Naturally participating in the LinkedIn Group community will provide you with opportunities to find others and be found, but here is some additional advice to consider in creating your own unique engagement strategy:

LIKING

Do you want to plant your face and name inside the group and be seen as an active participant, which could potentially make it easier for other group members to remember you? You can do this by "liking" a discussion. This simple action adds your photo to the front page of your group under the discussion tab, adds your photo and name to the activity feed of the group, and displays your name as someone who "liked" the discussion at the top of the actual discussion page. This can be especially effective if you do this for a conversation in which you think your target customer might be involved and/or a discussion you feel might become a hot topic within your group. You obviously want to pick and choose what you "like," but liking even one discussion a day can potentially help you become noticed by a lot of people and kick start new relationships with other group members.

COMMENTING

A comment in a group discussion can travel a great distance on LinkedIn. On every group homepage there is a dedicated space for the most popular discussions. For this discussion and all others, there is a link on the bottom right-hand corner of the discussion box that says, "see all xx comments." If you have something relevant to add to the discussion and end up commenting, chances are that those who commented before you will receive your comment via email if they've left the default setting of "send me an email for each new comment" checked when they submitted a comment. In this way, you can easily make a social impact on all of those who commented before you. This is an easy way to engage with many people as well as potentially indirectly market your product if the discussion topic is on target.

POSTING

Starting your own discussion is another great way to engage within a LinkedIn Group, especially if you ask a question or share compelling content that can yield a lot of engagement from other group members. Not only will your photo be prominently featured as the originator of the discussion (a distinction that could land your photo in the "Top Influencers This Week" widget) but everyone who participates in the discussion will indirectly be engaged in conversation with you. Depending on who engages with you, you just might find a future potential business partner or client commenting on the discussion you started.

SHARING

If there is a discussion you either started or you want others to see you engaged in, you can share the conversation outside of the group to encourage others to participate and hopefully discover you. While this is a feature that is available only in open groups, you can easily share the conversation on Twitter, your LinkedIn Status Update, or Facebook profile

CASE STUDY

Building a Business from LinkedIn Groups Engagement

If you recognize that LinkedIn is essentially a huge virtual networking event, there's no better place to rub elbows with your potential business partners and customers than in LinkedIn Groups. If you create your own system for developing relationships by spending time monitoring conversations and finding the most valuable components that could lead to potential business leads, you may find that LinkedIn can be a primary source for a great deal of your business.

BACKGROUND

James Filbird owns an international trading company based in Shenzhen, China.[1] After launching his company, Filbird had two issues to solve; his target customers and business partners were overseas, and he had no marketing budget. At that juncture, Filbird decided to invest in developing business using social media.

Over the past two years, China has consistently blocked access to Facebook, Twitter, and YouTube, but with the exception of a single day, LinkedIn has always been accessible behind the Chinese firewall. Furthermore, Filbird believed that of all of the social networking platforms, LinkedIn would be the best place to find others who had similar interests with whom he could network, and thus it became his sole online tool to grow his business.

WHAT HAPPENED

Armed with less than 100 connections, Filbird put his profile together in a way that represented the type of business for which he was looking. He has since spent one-and-a-half to two hours each day on the site viewing news on LinkedIn Today, checking his network updates, and keeping in touch with his current network. However, he spends the majority of his time with other members of the 50 LinkedIn Groups in which he is a member. He participates in many discussions and spends

---

1. http://www.jmftradegroup.com/

an additional hour of time each day scouring the daily digests of all of his LinkedIn Groups.

Over time, Filbird has learned to adjust his group membership so that he concentrates on relevant groups with large memberships and active discussions where he feels business might be looming. If he joins and finds these factors lacking, he looks for another group. Because of this, 70 percent of his group memberships have changed over the years, but one thing has stayed the same: For every ten discussions James engages in that he feels has business potential, one of them turns into actual business.

He begins by looking through the daily digest, then engages in the group, reaches out to connect, and then takes the conversation off of LinkedIn to Skype, where a deeper relationship can be cultivated. Every time LinkedIn has resulted in business, it has always been through this method.

SUMMARY

Filbird has been able to grow his business from scratch in the last three years to $5 million in annual revenue, and LinkedIn now accounts for 75 percent of that business. Though spending two-and-a-half to three hours a day on LinkedIn may sound like a lot, the ROI is definitely a positive one for him.

through the "share this discussion" functionality that appears in the top right-hand corner of the discussion.

Answers

LinkedIn Answers is one of the least used yet most popular engagement forums for business development on LinkedIn. Over the past several months we have seen the emergence of Quora,[46] a social networking platform purely focused on professional Q&A, as well as the addition

---

46. http://www.quora.com

of Questions to the Facebook platform where people can ask questions of their friends. To the credit of LinkedIn, the answers forum, which is a similar Q&A platform, has been an integral application on the site for several years. The latest statistic we have for how many questions exist on the answers forum is from May 2009, when LinkedIn indicated on its blog that there were more than 2 million cumulative answers.[47] This same blog post noted that the answers platform had grown by 1 million in just one year. At that rate, and with the overall growth of LinkedIn since then, it is easy to speculate that there might be more than 5 million cumulative answers currently in the answers forum.

To understand how to engage in LinkedIn Answers, it helps to under-stand why this growth of the public Q&A forum is happening. As we spend more and more time in social media, we now use it as one of our primary means of sourcing information. We used to pick up the phone or send out an email to ask similar questions, but now we can use forums like this one to ask many more (and potentially more qualified) people. Considering LinkedIn's professional demographic and the fact that the site has created categories that revolve around professional interests, it is only natural that this has become another social forum where those working in business-related fields have converged to engage with each other and ask experts for solutions to industry problems. You can post a discussion in a group and ask a targeted question there, or you can do so on the answers forum, which can then be answered by anyone on LinkedIn who considers himself or herself an expert as defined by the category in which you post your question.

The explanation I always give regarding the potential power of LinkedIn Answers for business development is through my own experience of posting a question about anti-virus software in the IT category. In less than 48 hours, I was overwhelmed with 69 answers, and most of those who answered were IT professionals along with a mix of engineers, sales and marketing professionals, and small-business owners. This is a classic example of the many business problems professionals have and those who

---

47. http://blog.linkedin.com/2009/05/05/happy-birthday-seis-anos-de-linkedin/

are stepping up to answer in a public forum to display their expertise—or potentially gain your business. I could have asked my close physical network for feedback, but as with social networking in general, the answer I would have received would have been limited by the experiences and diversity of those people I personally know. But what happens if you can ask a question to 100 million professionals, many of whom have much more expertise in certain areas than you do? That is the idea behind LinkedIn Answers, and that is why it continues to receive many questions that could lead to business for your company.

Before we take a closer look as to how sales and marketing professionals can engage in the answers forums to develop business and create connections of relevant value, let's look at the demographic and psyche of those asking the questions on LinkedIn. The people asking questions:

- Fall into a professional demographic
- Have, on average, a six–figure income[48]
- Are usually asking a question because they are looking for advice they can't find in their own physical network

Knowing these general characteristics of those asking questions on LinkedIn Answers puts you in a position to capitalize on potential business opportunities through this platform. In order to get the most out of answers, however, make sure you do the following:

OWN YOUR CATEGORY

LinkedIn currently has more than 22 categories into which the answers forums are organized, and some categories have multiple subcategories. The first thing you need to do is understand in which one(s) your target customer might be posting questions. Once you have that figured out, you need to "own" those categories. In order to own a category, you need to constantly monitor it and try to be one of the first to respond to those questions that are relevant to your business. Over time, this should add up

---

48. http://blog.linkedin.com/2007/12/18/top-10-ways-for/

to more visibility, Best Answers (which leads to expertise stars, explained below), and more leads found and business developed.

I recommend you make engagement on the answers platform part of your daily LinkedIn routine. You can do this efficiently by subscribing to the real-time RSS feed that LinkedIn provides for each category.

ENGAGE WITH THOSE ASKING THE QUESTIONS

The beauty about LinkedIn's public nature is that you can engage with the person asking the question regardless of your connectivity status by hitting the "reply privately" link that appears below any given question. In other words, if you have some top-secret information that you don't want to make public to your competitors, simply contact the professional with the business problem directly.

There are times when you will want to make your answer—enhanced with some reference links back to your website—public. But if you are looking to truly engage with the person asking the question in order to develop a business relationship, this private option provides the highest probability that you will receive a response in return.

ENGAGE WITH THOSE ANSWERING THE QUESTIONS

The fact that you answer the question in your own domain of expertise means there may be advantages in getting to know the person who asked the question—or even other people who answered the question. These are truly open and virtual forums for you to network with your peers. The question is merely the vehicle in which to do so. This is a great example of how you can leverage LinkedIn to engage with other business professionals who might be able to offer a complementary solution to the same business problem; thus the potential for a mutually beneficial business alliance is discovered.

REACH OUT TO THE EXPERTS

LinkedIn gives those whose answers are chosen as the "best" an expertise star, a designation that remains with them on their profile. These experts can be found (listed in descending order by the number of stars that they have received) on the front page of any given answers category. If you are trying to develop relationships with those working in organizations of a given industry represented by a category on LinkedIn Answers, you should be reaching out to the experts in that industry as represented by their answers track record. These are people who have already developed relationships with a lot of your potential customers simply by answering questions. Although you'll need to confirm so by looking at their profiles, their frequent use of answers may indicate that they are open to being contacted by you.

BECOMING AN EXPERT AND DISPLAYING YOUR EXPERTISE

Though your goal in engaging with the LinkedIn Answers forum should be to develop business and not necessarily become the expert for a certain category, simply answering a question not only shows off your expertise as well as that of the company you represent but also gives you exposure. Anyone who visits this question will see your profile headline. Although questions become automatically closed seven days after they are posted here, they live on forever in the answers database and may become indexed by search engines like Google as well. LinkedIn also gives you the option to display all of your questions and answers on your LinkedIn Profile, so if you answered a question that your potential customers commonly ask you, use this opportunity to display your expertise on your publicly visible profile.

ASKING A QUESTION

While there are stories of some who have developed business through asking a question, this will be covered in the section regarding gaining mindshare on LinkedIn in Chapter 10.

Network Updates

What I refer to in this book as the status update is simply the box that appears on your LinkedIn home page prompting you to share an update. As you've likely noticed, updates made by your connections, as well as their profile updates, group activity, answers activity, and even company updates have the potential to show up in the network updates listing on your home page, depending on their privacy settings.[49] Creating a daily LinkedIn routine provides the ability to engage with connections for potential business development opportunities, and scanning network updates should be part of that routine. There is no secret formula here, as you never know what updates from your network will be posted, but just as using Twitter Lists to navigate conversations on Twitter allows users to scan updates they might have otherwise missed, network updates provide a filter by your network that could reveal any of the following:

- A profile update that indicates someone is now working for a new company located in your territory
- A status update indicating someone is looking for a company for which yours offers the ideal expertise
- A comment on a LinkedIn Group discussion that could be relevant to your business but you might have missed because you're not a member of that group
- A response on the LinkedIn Answers board that could be relevant to your business
- A notice that someone in your network has started to follow a company that turns out to be an up-and-coming competitor, which triggers you to take an in-depth look at it

The beauty about engagement with network updates is that you simply need to contact your connection directly to get background information on the activity and see if there is a hidden business opportunity. It is by scanning this section of your homepage that you'll realize how having a targeted, industry-specific network yields hyper-specific network updates while a more diverse network yields information that you might have missed. That's why, when building out your network on LinkedIn, recognizing the importance of both of these types of connections is critical.

---

49. You can define who can see your "activity feed" as well as whether or not to turn on "activity broadcasts" under "privacy controls" in your profile settings.

One more thing to note is, just as you can engage with your connections based on their network updates, you too can spark engagement by updating your network regularly with what your current business needs are. There is no golden rule as to how often you should update your status update, but aim for a daily update to keep your network informed of how they can help you, how you can help them, your latest company news that might be relevant to them, and compelling industry news curated from other sources you think others might find interesting. Monitor how many of your connections engage with you on certain types of content in order to optimize the content mix of your status updates.

Events

LinkedIn Events is an optional application which you can and should install as it gives you access to a database of future as well as past events that can provide information on those people you might want to engage with to meet your business objectives. There are three ways to use the events application for engagement:

FINDING A PROFESSIONAL EVENT

You can actually use the online networking world of LinkedIn to help you find an *offline* business networking event that could help facilitate business development for your company. Although Facebook has an events application as well and event-centric sites such as Eventbrite[50] or Plancast[51] exist, only LinkedIn Events is concentrated on the professional demographic that includes B2B decision makers. With this in mind, use the search capabilities in this application to search for professional events your target customers might attend on a regular basis.

ENGAGING WITH ATTENDEES

By far the most valuable part of the events application is the ability to see who is attending or potentially interested in attending the event. You can

---

50. http://www.eventbrite.com/
51. http://www.plancast.com

CASE STUDY

The Importance of Relevant Status Updates

Many people tend to feed their Twitter updates into LinkedIn's status update field, but this space is more than just a place to throw out your latest thoughts. What you place in your status update permeates throughout your entire network, so be strategic about what you post here. Those who want to maintain mindshare will use this space to update their connections on current projects, conferences and workshops at which they are teaching or speaking, and expansions on their skills and offerings. If the right person sees the right status update at the right time, a business deal may be the end result.

BACKGROUND

Sue Henry[1] teaches basic social media classes and consistently does research to stay updated on the latest trends. She came across a few articles that noted the increase in online donations for nonprofits versus a decrease in other types of donations and wrote up a proposal that shared strategic tips and actions based on her "15 minutes a day for those who aren't 20-something anymore" method. Henry often uses her status update to share what she does and for whom she works, but she words her updates so they don't sound like a sales pitch. For this particular project, in which she'd simply written a proposal (and hadn't actually presented on the topic), Henry posted something along the lines of, "Just completed a proposal for a nonprofit that will help them increase online donations."

WHAT HAPPENED

Tom Schmoll, a fellow Business Network International director, had taken one of Henry's social media courses in the past. He saw her status update about the nonprofit proposal and recommended that Denise Laymon, who heads the NRF Conference (which encompasses more than 50 different nonprofits), check out what Henry had to offer via LinkedIn. He also told Laymon that Henry was teaching a class in Grand Rapids (about five hours north of Henry's home) for a chamber/college co-initiative. Laymon attended the class (though Henry still didn't know

---

1. http://www.suehenrytalks.com

her) and contacted her on LinkedIn after that. The two communicated via messages on LinkedIn; the conversation then moved to a phone interview.

SUMMARY
Until he saw the status update, Schmoll was unaware that Henry was interested in working with nonprofit organizations, but based on that simple message that went out to her entire network, Henry's phone interview turned into a speaking opportunity. She was booked to provide a two-hour training at the NRF regional conference in St. James, North Dakota, in April 2010 which resulted in $1,200.00 of business from a combination of speaking fees, home study courses sales, and phone consultations.

scan the RSVP list and reach out to attendees in advance to try to schedule time to meet. In other words, instead of contacting others before a big industry event asking if they will be attending or hoping you will run into someone on the trade floor, LinkedIn Events gives you the ability to engage before the actual event, which increases the chances you will be able to schedule a meeting. This helps with person-to-person engagement because you already used LinkedIn to begin establishing a relationship.

SEARCHING PAST EVENTS

In addition to finding upcoming events to attend, you can also see who has attended past events. This can be useful if you just started using this application or are targeting a new industry. See who attended previous events and reach out to relevant people. The fact that they RSVP'd using the events application means they are invested in LinkedIn and are more apt to respond to your engagement because they find value in the platform.

Reading List by Amazon

I mentioned at the beginning of this chapter that some out-of-the-box thinking about engagement could yield actionable data on LinkedIn.

LinkedIn's Reading List by Amazon is one such example. This is an application you can display on your profile that informs your network of books you have read (with an option to recommend them to your network), are currently reading, or intend to read. Obviously if you don't read many books this may not be of a lot of value, but assuming you are a frequent book reader simply because you are reading this book, check out the engagement potential this application holds:

INDUSTRY UPDATES

One of the default tabs for this application is the ability to display updates of who is reading what from the industry you selected for your profile. Look at the profiles of people displayed here and see if any are in your target market. Initial engagement begins with "watching" their reading lists so your name appears when they see who is following their list. If you notice someone is reading a book you have also read, this could be an excellent conversation starter in sparking professional engagement.

COMMON BOOKS READ

The other way of finding those on LinkedIn who have read the same book that you have, regardless of the industry they've selected, is to simply click the title of any book that you have added to your own reading list in the application and scan the section "what people are saying about this book" for those people you might want to contact. Use this common book as a vehicle of engagement. This might not work for everyone, but like everything else in social media, the more you are authentically committed to the community and relevant in your communication, the better your chances in achieving successful engagement.

I covered additional applications and forums more thoroughly in *Windmill Networking: Maximizing LinkedIn,* but with a little creative thinking, you should be able to utilize the plethora of targeted engagement opportunities provided by LinkedIn.

Utilizing Business Intelligence from the Professional Graph

CHAPTER OBJECTIVES

▦ *Learn how to specifically gather business intelligence from LinkedIn's applications and platforms*

▦ *Explore the opportunities for intelligence gathering specifically for LinkedIn Signal and LinkedIn Today*

▦ *Provide context for what is in a user profile and how that can assist with business*

▦ *Understand the importance of LinkedIn Answers in finding potential business opportunities*

WHILE MOST MARKETERS CONCENTRATE ON FACEBOOK AND the so-called "social graph," which helps map out who is friends with whom and what personal interests they have that could make them potential customers, fans, or even brand advocates of your company's products, the social graph breaks down for most B2B companies. Why? Because these same people are, in most cases, not consuming the products and services that their company makes. This isn't to say that business intelligence from people can't be culled from Facebook, because it can, but LinkedIn's extensive business-oriented features provide a more thorough snapshot of the professional demographic. I use the term "professional graph" to contrast what LinkedIn offers in comparison to Facebook. This professional graph, which is created using data from the

100 million members of LinkedIn, allows business professionals to cull the following information from LinkedIn in comparison to Facebook:

- Where they went to school (also on Facebook)
- Where they work (recently enhanced on Facebook but potentially not as detailed as on LinkedIn)
- Who recommends them
- Who is in their professional network
- What professional dialogue they are having
- What industry or business books they are reading
- What business events they are attending

The list goes on and on, but the point is that there is a tremendous amount of information available on LinkedIn that can be utilized as business intelligence for your company's sales and marketing professionals. While resources such as Hoovers and OneSource offer business information, they don't come close to providing nearly as much detailed information on the professional graph nor do they offer the applications and tools LinkedIn provides to reach out for business development. We've covered some of LinkedIn's applications and forums in previous chapters; now it's time to learn how to cull business intelligence about companies, industries, and professionals using tools available with the free account.

LinkedIn Companies

We discussed LinkedIn's Companies page in detail in Chapter 5, but let's examine how to use this tool to find business intelligence on the company pages of our target customers and competitors. Though the amount of information on these pages does not rival that of the previously mentioned business information services, it does offer a snapshot of data culled from the professional graph that can assist in sales and marketing efforts not available on those other sites.

YOUR NETWORK

Your own professional graph is based on your LinkedIn network, and on the front page of every LinkedIn Companies Page, you can see who in your network works at that company as well as pictures of those who connect you to second-degree connections working there. In other words, instead of doing an advanced people search for that company, you can simply go to a company's page and find all of the aggregated information there. Viewing a company's page also indicates if any of your connections recently began working at the company.

NEW HIRES

New hires are given a contract for a reason, and these new employees, especially if they are at the decision-making level of an organization, potentially yield influence in the direction that the organization is moving. Where did these new hires come from? What were their past titles and what are their present ones? Analysis of this information can provide business intelligence as well as help target those who might be interested in giving your company's products a second chance, especially if they were hired to change things.

FOLLOWERS

Just as viewing who follows whom on Twitter is available to the public, you can also see who is following any given company on LinkedIn. Many people follow companies for real-time updates regarding job openings, but there could be competitors with which you're unfamiliar or potential non-competing marketing partners from other industries following the company as well. Use this intelligence gleaned from followers to do more research or engage.

All of the above information comes from the front page for any given company. More intelligence can be found by selecting "check out insightful statistics about (Company Name) employees" near the top right-hand corner of a company's page. On this next page we can see the following information:

PEOPLE ALSO VIEWED

This may alert you to new potential customers or competitors who might have been under the radar but are now exposed due to analyzing the viewing habits of LinkedIn users who visited this company's page.

NEW TITLES AND DEPARTURES

I recently spoke for a commercial real estate company's annual sales conference and, to the shock of those in attendance, congratulated its new vice president of operations, and noted that she had been promoted internally from another department where she had been a director even though I'd never met her. I culled this information from the "new titles" tab for this specific business on LinkedIn Companies. Following changes within an organization was, up until the advent of LinkedIn, impossible to track, so this public business intelligence regarding the inner organizational changes of any given company is invaluable. Perhaps a new title was given to someone because a new organization was created within the company that falls into your target market. Utilize the intelligence of those who departed the company for similar information as well as other details on their recent employer. Non-disclosure agreements (NDAs) restrict information they can provide, but without a doubt they have solid internal relationships that can potentially be utilized to help map out the organization.

MOST RECOMMENDED

These are the people within the company that have received the most recommendations. If I am trying to get my foot in the door at a particular company where I don't know anyone, this is where I look. Why? Though there's no proof behind the theory, many people who have a lot of recommendations on their LinkedIn profiles may have at some time been in transition and became heavy LinkedIn users. They are also probably experienced networkers, so if you want to "network" your way into an organization, try contacting these people first.

SERVICES RECOMMENDATIONS

If a company you are targeting has a products and/or services tab, see if it has received any recommendations. While it is easy to simply "follow" a company without much emotion or potential for damaging your reputation, professionals who post recommendations on products or services listed on LinkedIn are truly putting their professional reputations on the line. These people might not be easy to contact if you don't know them, but this offers a picture of whom your competitor's fans are and what they like about the company if they left comments. When you view the products and services tab, check to see if anyone in your network is connected to a true fan of the company; this information cannot be found using an advanced people search.

In addition to what is noted above, there is other business intelligence to be gleaned from the LinkedIn Companies Page. For instance, a common problem is if you are targeting a Fortune 500 client or similar organization with thousands or tens of thousands of employees but you don't have any first- or second-degree connections nor do you know the exact decision maker you want to contact on LinkedIn. In other words, you want to "work" the professional graph but don't know where to start. Filters on a company's page, such as university attended, former and current employers, and where employees call home all help in organization navigation and provide hints on how to effectively target your advanced people search.

Follow Your Competition

There are many reasons why you should want to follow your competition on LinkedIn:

- It provides insight on when new employees come and go as well as when internal promotions take place. A sales person's understanding of a client's organization is critical intelligence, and following companies on LinkedIn is the best source of public information available in this respect.
- New job openings may hint at strengths or weaknesses in a particular product division—or reveal marketing intelligence of entry into a new market based on the title advertised. You can also get information on

any updates your competition makes to its current company page, which allows you to stay in touch with what is going on in its marketing department.

- Sales managers are always taking note of the most talented sales professionals to tap for future growth. Following your competitor might give you a hint as to when that star salesperson you've been monitoring has left the competition and may be available to join your firm.

Following your competition is easy. Simply conduct a companies search and follow specific companies by selecting the appropriate icon in the top right-hand corner of the overview page. You can then choose to opt-in to daily or weekly updates from all of the companies you follow via email by accessing your notification settings located beneath the "following" tab on the companies page. Start by receiving daily digests, and if you don't see any value in them, switch to weekly digests. All it takes is one bit of data from the competition to spark your company's sales and marketing efforts.

LinkedIn Signal

LinkedIn Signal is a business intelligence tool that most LinkedIn users have never heard of. The reason is simple; this application appears nowhere in the user interface of LinkedIn.com. Instead, it is featured on LinkedIn Labs, a separate website which, in LinkedIn's words, "hosts a small set of projects and experimental features built by the employees of LinkedIn. We share them here as demonstrations and to solicit feedback, but please remember that they are intended to be low-maintenance experiments, and may be added and removed over time based on popularity and support."[52] We'll only discuss Signal here, but I advise you periodically check out other applications that appear here to see if they have any business value.

Start by accessing Signal here: http://www.linkedin.com/signal/

Signal can be visually overwhelming in its detail at first, but it truly is a powerful tool that provides a LinkedIn filter from which to view the status updates of *all* LinkedIn users. All Twitter tweets integrated into LinkedIn

---

52. http://www.linkedinlabs.com/

profiles as well as LinkedIn Status Updates themselves from your extended LinkedIn network as well as those that aren't even part of your network are searchable here via a number of filters. The user interface is easy to navigate, with search filters on the left, timeline in the middle, and trending links on the right.

What seems extremely simple is actually very powerful for the following reason: LinkedIn, based on profiles with professional demographic data, is very much a closed social networking site that is relationship-centric, while Twitter, displaying little bio information about any given user but a lot of what they think about, is an open social networking site that is idea-centric. Signal brings these two worlds together, allowing the data to commingle in a compelling way. Let's take a look at some specific scenarios that illustrate the potential of how you can use targeted searches on LinkedIn Signal to hunt for targeted business intelligence for your company:

FIND POTENTIAL CUSTOMERS

You could find potential new customers on Signal just by searching the conversations. Search for any given keyword and you'll see who is talking about the subject that is relevant to your business or retweeting trending information in your industry. Use Signal to filter the business intelligence contained in these tweets and status updates with the professional graph provided by LinkedIn.

TARGET TWITTER USERS WITHIN A COMPANY

By far the most valuable part of Signal is the ability to see who at a particular company is tweeting. The Signal algorithm appears to only use the most current company listed on any given profile, so if you are looking for business intelligence about a particular company, you might be able to glean interesting data by looking at tweets from current employees. If you want to connect with someone from a particular company for business development purposes, it might be easier to begin engagement with those LinkedIn users that are already active on Twitter rather than seek out an introduction from a LinkedIn user, especially if your potential connection is three degrees of separation or more away from you. Twitter is a relatively flat society when compared to LinkedIn, so use the intelligence gleaned from Signal to provide information and data points to facilitate networking on both platforms. You decide which social media channel is best for engagement with any given person and/or situation.

HASHTAG ANALYSIS

Hashtags classify tweets so users and search engines can find them when the wording of a tweet does not necessarily contain the keywords of your message. Signal shows the most popular hashtags associated with tweets from your LinkedIn connections and for any given keyword searched in the bottom right-hand section of the filters called "topics." This can help you better utilize hashtags for your own tweets as well as figure out the most popular hashtags to search for yourself. Your marketing division can use this invaluable tool to optimize hashtag utilization in future tweets.

CONTENT CURATION

B2B social media marketing often requires curating content—or sourcing third-party content to share with your social media network and followers—to maintain mindshare, spark engagement, and be perceived as a subject matter expert. While there are many tools that exist outside of LinkedIn to help achieve this, Signal is another tool to add to that list. In addition to being able to search the public status updates of LinkedIn users, Signal's advantage as a Twitter search engine is that it finds relevant tweets for any given keyword from within the professional graph. Narrow the results to your first-degree connections as well as how long ago the tweet was sent and combine this with the trending links for several ideas on content your followers might find interesting. LinkedIn, of course, makes it easy to now share that content within its platform with a "share" button below any tweet that includes a link already embedded into the status update.

TWEETS

LinkedIn also provides an optional application called Tweets that allows you to monitor the tweets of only your first-degree connections. Because

LinkedIn Signal already has this functionality and much more, it might not become your primary tool for mining business intelligence data from tweets, but Tweets provides the professional two important functional components that can help in analyzing conversation from your LinkedIn connections:

1. The ability to see all of your connections who are on LinkedIn and directly follow them from within the Tweets application if you are not already doing so
2. The ability to create a Twitter list of only your LinkedIn connections so that you can now easily monitor their tweets when on Twitter. Note that Twitter limits the number of followers on any given list to 500, so if you are a super connector or avid networker, the list might only be a partial collection

LinkedIn Today

LinkedIn Today, which appears under the news tab in the top menu bar, represents the power and value of the professional graph. We all consume information online yet are often confused about where to find relevant information because of the democratization of content creation and distribution. We try to follow others on Twitter, StumbleUpon, Delicious, and Digg, and we join LinkedIn Groups and follow pages to find sources of information that are relevant to us. Though we still need to think about those things, LinkedIn Today is a user-generated and customizable online newspaper that could be valuable to active social media users who consume lots of information on a daily basis. The information contained here also provides us invaluable business intelligence for multiple objectives.

LinkedIn Signal is powerful because we can search tweets and status updates that are created from within the LinkedIn community and filter them through the professional graph as presented by our specific searches in an advanced people search. Signal helps sort through who on LinkedIn is talking about what and then uses that information to connect with them on LinkedIn or Twitter. LinkedIn Today takes the actual content of a shared link and displays the most popular news shared on LinkedIn and Twitter (based on LinkedIn users who have integrated their Twitter profiles) by industry. This means, for example, that if I am in the online media industry, I can cut through the clutter of conversations on social media sites and simply see the news that is most shared by LinkedIn users in my industry. In other words, I can read the information that LinkedIn's professional graph has determined important to any given industry—an important filter that saves time and provides relevant business information.

LinkedIn Today offers the following features that make it a compelling tool for targeted business intelligence:

CONTENT CURATION

The potential for sourcing content as part of your social media marketing program is plentiful within this application:

- The top five most-shared articles from all of the industries and sources you follow conveniently appear at the top of the page.
- Headlines below this module are the top five most-shared articles from professionals within each of the industries that you follow.
- Selecting "see all" from any industry either from within each industry news module or on the top navigation bar (conveniently updated with industries you follow as well as those in which LinkedIn feels you might be interested) shows the top ten most-shared articles by professionals from within that industry.
- A widget powered by StumbleUpon,[53] which reads "discover more in xx," located just below the fold in the middle of the page in any given industry, shows the most popular reads from this social bookmarking service that might not have appeared on Today.
- Additional widgets appear below the StumbleUpon one for "novel & newsworthy" as well as a module "from your connections," which provides even more news.

---

53. http://www.stumbleupon.com/stumbler/nealschaffer

By following sources and industries relevant to your company and scanning the content that appears in the locations noted above, you can grasp at a glance what content is popular. If you're looking for content to share in your LinkedIn Group or Status Update, anything that appears here is a good choice, but if content is too popular, find the most recent post or story related to that news to share with your followers and other LinkedIn users. To make your content curation complete, for any article that you read, you now have the ability to share it on LinkedIn directly by selecting the appropriate icons in each article summary.

UNDERSTANDING THE NEEDS OF YOUR TARGET CUSTOMER

You can see who and how many people shared a particular news item from LinkedIn Today. If you click on the blue wraparound icon with the number, you will see a screen with information on who shared this headline. Looking through this information allows you to see who shared it, read comments they made about it, and search through the people who shared it by company, industry, or location. Using this tool, we can see what type of content resonates with whom and why, which provides valuable business intelligence for marketing efforts. Business development professionals might also find a way to engage potential customers simply by "liking" or sharing content they've posted.

User Profile Data

One of the best sources of business intelligence is the actual data included on the user profile of any given company employee. Though not every employee fills out the profile as much as we'd like to see for business intelligence, the following information can be potentially gleaned from scanning someone's profile:

- Professional background → Look for where professional graphs might overlap.
- Educational background → Look for where professional graphs might overlap.

- Who has recommended them and what the recommendation says ⇢ Look for potentially important data here. Check to see if you are connected in any way to the professional who wrote the recommendation.
- Professional connections (if we are connected with them and they allow others to browse their connections) ⇢ Look for connections who are also potential customers.
- Professional specialties ⇢ Check to see if these align with your company's products.
- Interests ⇢ Look for anything that allows you to spark a conversation.
- Groups and Associations ⇢ Look for any professional associations outside of LinkedIn or LinkedIn Groups through which you can connect. Perhaps you should become a member of the same LinkedIn Groups.
- Viewers of This Profile Also Viewed ⇢ Check for any other potential customers here.

LinkedIn Groups and Answers

Discussions in LinkedIn Groups and questions in LinkedIn Answers can also provide business intelligence by showing what problems those in the industry are facing and how other companies or professionals are responding to them. In addition to engaging with others for potential business purposes in these forums, we can also gather qualitative marketing data. These public LinkedIn forums combined with analyses of public conversations from Twitter and status updates through Signal and Today help us stay on top of industry news and trends for a wide variety of purposes. Ultimately, this intelligence can help us better market our products and services.

Advice on Prospecting on LinkedIn

CHAPTER OBJECTIVES
- *Learn strategies for connecting with those who are difficult to find and contact on LinkedIn*
- *Understand how to use the LinkedIn Profile Organizer to better organize profiles of business prospects*

THIS BOOK HAS PROVIDED SUGGESTIONS ON FINDING AND engaging with your target customers on LinkedIn. It has also discussed how to cull business intelligence from the applications provided by LinkedIn. Together, these tools provide information on how to start a conversation with a prospective customer or client. The next challenge in prospecting on LinkedIn is how to find and contact those who are difficult to contact on the site. This advice echoes the section in Chapter 4 called Connecting with People Outside of Your Network, but takes a broader look at various tools LinkedIn provides to aid in communication with your prospects.

Reaching the "Untouchables"

Though LinkedIn is a virtual trade show, there are those who attend industry exhibitions but don't spend time on the floor or in the breakout sessions. These may be executives who registered for the show yet spend their time in private VIP suites meeting with customers only by invitation. If your efforts until now have not allowed you to gain access to those key decision makers behind locked doors, there are many innovative ways to reach out beyond your first-degree connections on LinkedIn.

INTRODUCTIONS

Your highest degree of success in reaching out to someone you don't know in the business world is through a warm introduction, and LinkedIn has an introduction feature that allows you to request an introduction from someone either directly or indirectly connected to that person. You can have five outstanding default introductions at any given time with the free account, so be strategic in how you utilize them. If the person you want to contact is a second-degree connection and you know the person that connects you very well, your chances of being able to contact this person are very high. However, if the person you want to contact is a third-degree connection, you can choose the first-degree connection who will receive the introduction request to forward, but you can't control the "missing link"—the second-degree connection. This greatly decreases your chances for success in connecting with your desired contact.

Despite the buzz about online social media marketing, B2B business is still often an offline social event. If the key person you want to contact is a third-degree connection, pick up the phone and ask your first-degree connection if he or she could contact your second-degree connection and potentially facilitate an introduction. Asking for a warm introduction the old-fashioned way is by far the most effective way to successfully introduce yourself to someone else.

JOIN THE SAME GROUP

A ninja tactic that many savvy sales and marketing professionals utilize is joining the same LinkedIn Group specifically to contact a certain member.

The default setting for groups is to allow others in the group to message you regardless of your connectivity status. However, some people don't want to be contacted and change this setting, so this strategy may not work 100 percent of the time.

MONITOR GROUP ACTIVITY

You may be limited to how much information you can see on people's profiles if you are not directly connected with them. Joining the same group as these people allows you to see more of their activity and also gives you one more potential way to contact them: through a Group discussion. While this feature is commonly referred to as the "follow" feature, you don't necessarily have to follow that prospect. Simply find that person in the members tab for any particular group and you will find a "see activity" link under any given name. If that person has posted a discussion or comment to any group of which you are a member, you can now engage with him or her in a virtual discussion and build rapport in this manner. This is a good option for those who would prefer to naturally engage in a discussion versus openly sending a message.

"WORK" THE PROFILE

Look very carefully at the profiles belonging to the people with whom you want to connect. If they have LinkedIn applications installed, you may be able to get in touch through those platforms. If they RSVP to a LinkedIn Event, attend the event. If they display their blog, comment on the blog. If they ask a question on LinkedIn Answers, answer it. Check the profile for a phone number, email address, or link to a website that may allow you to contact them off of LinkedIn.

TWITTER

If you notice that your target second- or third-degree contact is on Twitter, which may be noted on the LinkedIn profile, take advantage of the hyper-social nature of Twitter and send an @Reply message. If you feel that is too direct, retweet their content and/or add them to a Twitter list, both of which are indirect ways that could spark natural engagement.

CASE STUDY

High Quality LinkedIn Network Fosters Successful Prospecting

Expanding your network on LinkedIn is not merely about amassing a large number of contacts. It is about adding high-quality contacts that increase the number of data points connecting you with decision makers at target companies. Just as recommendations add credibility to your profile, being connected with more relevant people increases your credibility and raises your reputation as defined by those with whom you are connected.

BACKGROUND

In 2005, Hervé Bloch[1] was a managing partner in a start-up company that provided content management system solutions and website creation for large companies and organizations. He was in charge of marketing, communication, and sales activities. Bloch discovered Viadeo (LinkedIn's French competitor), realized that a social networking platform had the potential to accelerate the process to close business deals and became one of the first users with more than 1,000 connections. A year later, he discovered LinkedIn, which he realized was global and more oriented toward decision makers. He began using the advanced people search feature to focus on the important contacts he had to make. Through the introduction function, he was able to make contact with people before getting in touch by phone, thus eliminating the need to cold call anyone.

WHAT HAPPENED

In 2008, Bloch was a regional manager at Emailvision (an email service provider) in charge of Central and East Europe with a focus on Switzerland, Germany, and the Russian Federation. He recruited and managed teams in Geneva, Zurich, Hamburg, and Munich. Before launching an office in the Russian Federation, Bloch had to close the first business deal, so he used the advanced people search feature on

---

1. http://www.linkedin.com/in/hervebloch

LinkedIn to find five priority prospects. He engaged in conversation and closed a deal with Woman Journal without ever traveling to his client's location. The important component of the business, however, was the fact that he had 18 contacts in common with his client, which helped settle any doubts about Bloch's legitimacy.

SUMMARY

LinkedIn in particular and professional social networking in general convinced Bloch to launch his own company Digilinx.[2] He has more than 3,600 direct connections, and it is an extremely important tool in his business. More than 70 percent or 6 million (nearly US$9 million) of his business is generated from the site.

2. http://www.digilinx.fr/

THE MIGHTY INMAIL

As mentioned in Chapter 4, the "Hail Mary," $10-a-pop InMail is really your final if-everything-else-fails option. LinkedIn guarantees that it will reach the individual to whom you send it, and if you don't receive a response within seven days, you'll receive a replacement InMail. Because of the guaranteed delivery and the need to pay in order to send one, LinkedIn says that InMails generate a response rate that is 30 times greater than traditional email methods.[54]

Unfortunately, those that are least active on LinkedIn are the hardest people to reach. Many people on LinkedIn aren't involved in any groups and don't actively participate on others parts of the site. If you want to reach these people, sending an InMail or resorting to the classic networking method of calling a connection and asking for an introduction may be the best options for reaching your target person. Before you do either of these, however, use LinkedIn to do as much research as possible to increase your chances of success.

54. http://www.linkedin.com/static?key=promo_inmail_intro&trk=msitebd

Organizing Your Prospects with Profile Organizer

LinkedIn provides a tool only available to paid subscribers that should be mentioned here if you plan to use LinkedIn for prospecting: the Profile Organizer (this and other paid options will be covered in more detail in Chapter 13).

The LinkedIn Profile Organizer is a simple user interface that, if you are a paid member, will appear under the "profile" tab in the menu bar. As its name implies, you can organize any profiles on LinkedIn by saving them to specific folders (either 5 or 25 of them, depending on how much you pay). Once saved, you can add notes and contact details to the profile. You can do this for any profile on LinkedIn, regardless if they are first-degree connections or not.

Let's put this in perspective; if you are connected to people, you can already see their contact details and display notes in the contact information module on the right-hand side of a first-degree connection's profile. You can put your first-degree connection profiles in folders using LinkedIn Profile Organizer, but you can already tag and organize your contacts to some degree using this feature in the "my connections" application found under the contacts tab. The killer value of Profile Organizer for those who are actively prospecting on LinkedIn on a daily basis is the ability to organize profiles by saving them into virtual folders and write notes on those profiles to which you are not connected. The ability to organize prospects regardless of your connectivity status can save lots of precious time over months, as you can easily add those you find in an advanced people search into a virtual folder for prospects right from the search results screen.

Obtaining Thought Leadership and Gaining Mindshare on LinkedIn

---

CHAPTER OBJECTIVES

■ *Understand how promoting others' content can help gain mindshare and thought leadership on LinkedIn*

■ *Understand which LinkedIn Group discussions may reach the most people*

■ *Learn how to lead and participate in group discussions using third-party content to gain mindshare*

■ *Learn how to utilize LinkedIn Answers by asking questions you know the answers to in order to establish expertise and become an industry leader on LinkedIn*

UCCESSFUL SOCIAL MEDIA MARKETING REQUIRES BEING WHERE your audience is, frequenting appropriate social media channels such as LinkedIn, and engaging with platform users. These strategies give businesses and professionals the opportunity to gain the mindshare of potential clients if used correctly. Becoming the top-of-mind service provider for prospective customers makes your business the natural place to turn to when they need your particular product or service. In the past, many companies spent top marketing dollars to exhibit at trade shows and advertise in targeted industry magazines, but the ROI of these efforts may be decreasing because more people are simply spending their time elsewhere. Without a doubt, the trend of spending more time online, particularly on social media websites, is partially the cause. Instead of viewing this as a loss of market share, savvy companies are turning to social media such as LinkedIn to gain mindshare…and they're getting it for free simply by contributing and participating.

Social media allows both creators and curators of content to gain mindshare and thought leadership simply by being active participants in conversations and contributors who share branded and relevant content. Though it is sometimes appropriate to share content from your corporate website (a topic covered in depth in Chapter 11), you also need to share content created by others so you appear to be an objective and trustworthy industry expert and thought leader. Social media is not about self promotion, and those that only promote themselves often see their acts backfire.

This chapter considers the value of curating third parties' content and the importance of engaging in public forums on behalf of your company, but without the direct intent of leading them to your website at every chance, as a way to efficiently gain mindshare in social media and potentially even achieve thought leadership status on behalf of your company.

In order to capture the best audience for gaining mindshare with third-party content, the sales, marketing, and business development professionals in your company should focus the majority of their efforts on the public-facing areas of LinkedIn. It is in these areas that obtaining mindshare and eventual thought leadership are most likely to help generate future businesses, both directly and indirectly, simply because the exposure of potential customer engagement reaches many more people.

Status Updates

Just as tweets on Twitter can be a powerful way of sharing information, so can the LinkedIn Status Update. Though only your LinkedIn connections will see your status update in their network updates, you can display your status update for public visibility so that those who view your profile but are not connections can see what you are saying as well. Obviously LinkedIn is not Twitter and therefore it is not quantity of updates but quality and professional relevance that matters most. Try to aim at providing one update a day that contains information you find compelling or noteworthy about your company or industry that is of interest to your target market. When attaching a link to an update, import the relevant accompanying photos from the originating web site for eye-catching appeal if possible.

Groups

As mentioned earlier in this book, LinkedIn Groups contain the largest public audience to engage with on LinkedIn in order to gain mindshare. You do this not only by submitting your own content but also by sharing resourceful content in which related industry professionals might be interested and by providing your own interpretation or asking a question to spark a new conversation beyond the content shared. Providing third-party content (and not as much of your own) over an extended period of time in relevant groups helps you build trustworthy relationships with group members. While this may seem counterintuitive, it is similar to a rule that many have on Twitter; only send out a self-promotional tweet 10 or 20 percent of the time. You can and should promote yourself and your company occasionally on LinkedIn, but utilizing other functionalities on the site allows for better opportunities to do so. In order to maximize your LinkedIn Groups mindshare, join 50 groups (the maximum allowed by LinkedIn) and then start your own conversations as well as participate in those discussions started by others. To gain mindshare once you've joined a new group, check out the conversations and corresponding comments in the section highlighting the most popular discussions. If those who already commented have subscribed to receive follow-up comments by email, you can make a quick splash by adding a relevant and thought-provoking comment to the discussion, which is then sent to hundreds or thousands of people. For instance, some large groups have discussions that have already gathered dozens of comments. There are potentially hundreds of LinkedIn users who have subscribed to these comments, so your comment may be read by more people than an average tweet is. Contributing to the ever popular "introduce yourself" discussion posts is another easy way to discreetly and professionally note your expertise and start to build rapport with other group members.

CASE STUDY

Targeting the Wealthy B2C Consumer through LinkedIn Status Updates

Though the emphasis of this book is on selling products and services to other businesses, don't forget that the people working behind the companies on LinkedIn are also consumers, and wealthy consumers at that. If you have a product that is perfect for the LinkedIn demographic, put your network to use to help spread the word about your offerings. You might be pleasantly surprised with what LinkedIn can do for your B2C business.

BACKGROUND

Peter Taliangis,[1] based in Perth, Australia, was invited to join LinkedIn in 2006, and as an early adopter of technology he knew that establishing a robust LinkedIn profile was akin to having your own website. He became a real estate sales representative less than two years ago and has naturally continued to find a way to use LinkedIn for his business.

WHAT HAPPENED

Peter made it a habit to announce to his ever-growing network of local business professionals any new real estate listing of his through his status updates on LinkedIn. "When you list a property, you need lots of people to see it," Taliangis said. "You never know who might buy the property, so it is a very valuable tool. I post it in my status that goes to 1,800 people or so. If someone likes it, shares it, or similar, obviously more people will see it."

One day Taliangis was contacted by Kate and Chris Quinn, whom he had never met before. They had found him on LinkedIn and were impressed with how proactive he was in promoting his properties on the site. As a result, they gave Taliangis their listing.

SUMMARY

Taliangis promoted the Quinns' listing as he does all of his others via his status update on LinkedIn and received an immediate inquiry. He ended up selling the $300,000 Western Australia property before its first open house. Although he only netted $6,000 in commission, Taliangis'

---

1. http://www.linkedin.com/in/petertaliangis

clients were so thrilled with the results that they have referred clients to him ever since, so it's been worth much more than that.

"As for LinkedIn generally, it is my number one source for referrals, plus my number one source for promoting myself, my brand, and my business," Taliangis said. "It will only become more valuable the more I work the network, the connections, and the opportunities."

Overall, Taliangis estimates that the network he has built on LinkedIn has generated more than $300,000 of business.

Needless to say, it requires time and effort to create and foster relationships online just as it does in person. Constant interaction on discussions that provide educational, resourceful, and helpful information to others and posting links to third-party content shows that you want to add value as an industry expert to the conversation, not just dominate it with your own material. Sometimes starting discussions is the best way to show off your expertise. This can be done in two ways: sharing content you think other group members might be interested in with your own interpretation of why the news is important while at the same time trying to spark engagement from others, or starting a discussion on a topic that is currently being debated in your industry so that you can be the thought leader behind these ground-breaking revelations. In addition, spend time browsing discussions that others have started and add thoughtful comments where appropriate. This shows you are a leader but also willing to listen and engage with what others have to say. When everyone at your company engages in this practice, your business is more likely to be found on LinkedIn.

Answers

LinkedIn Answers is another public forum on which to share your expertise. Compared to the nearly one million LinkedIn Groups that exists, LinkedIn Answers is divided into only tens of categories and sub-categories. This mere classification of subject matter makes it easy to hone in on your target audience by constantly participating on the answer boards and responding to any or all questions that pertain to your area of expertise. Engagement on LinkedIn Answers could also lead to direct business, but the immediate and ongoing goal should be to establish your company's mindshare and thought leadership by ensuring that you and your employees are actively providing solutions or engaging thoughtfully with the questions posed by others.

You can also used LinkedIn Answers to post your own questions, thus sparking engagement and providing the opportunity to display your expertise. Posing a question that is intelligently written and speaks to the main issues your clients have gives you a chance to engage with the professionals who answer, potentially resulting in lead generation. Though many businesses with real problems pose questions on LinkedIn Answers, taking the opposite approach of asking a question when you know the answer is an excellent way to help build your thought leadership because everyone is responding to the question presented from your profile, which is referenced every time a LinkedIn user reads the question.

Polls

Asking a question relevant to your industry using a poll is another great way to spark engagement from LinkedIn users who might not be active in groups or answers but might respond to a poll. In doing so, they may be inclined to look at the profile or company name of the user who submitted the poll. The subject matter of the poll may spark engagement on an issue that speaks to a pain point of your target market. Using polls is the easiest and one of the most enjoyable ways to engage your target LinkedIn professionals because public comments aren't necessary. When people take the poll, you will be able to see some demographic detail on who provided which answers. In order to gain mindshare using polls, you need to phrase your question in a way that makes your target audience interested in responding and/or viewing the results. If engagement is lacking, send the poll to your industry partners for feedback or promote the poll on other social media channels and/or your website, a topic discussed in Chapter 11.

Utilizing LinkedIn for Social Media Optimization

CHAPTER OBJECTIVES

▨ *Learn how to optimize your LinkedIn profile and status update for marketing purposes*

▨ *Understand best practices for utilizing LinkedIn Groups for social media optimization*

▨ *Determine which LinkedIn Applications are most applicable to your marketing strategies for social media optimization purposes*

▨ *Understand the relationship between your company's website and LinkedIn in regard to social media optimization*

SOCIAL MEDIA DOES NOT EXIST IN A VACUUM INSIDE YOUR organization. As such, LinkedIn should be completely integrated with all other social media marketing efforts. Social media optimization (SMO) is defined as using social media activities to attract unique visitors to your website content,[55] and LinkedIn allows users to do this both directly on LinkedIn as well as indirectly through other social media properties.

We discussed how to use social media to promote your LinkedIn Group earlier, but you can also use LinkedIn to promote your social media presence in general, therefore attracting more people from both LinkedIn and other social media platforms to your website. If your company is active

---

55. http://en.wikipedia.org/wiki/Social_media_optimization

on several social media platforms, you can also utilize LinkedIn to drive potential customers to these other sites as part of your LinkedIn-related marketing efforts.

Though previous chapters explained how to utilize different components of LinkedIn in detail, this chapter explains how to maximize them for your SMO. It also introduces optional applications available on LinkedIn for this very purpose.

Your LinkedIn Profile

There are three places to optimize your personal profile and the profiles of your employees:

Websites

Users can list up to three websites in this area. This is an obvious place for potential customers to find a company's website, and yet many small-business owners fail to include their company's URL here. Furthermore, you can customize the anchor text describing the link by selecting "other" from the type of websites. Though the SEO value of utilizing this feature is questionable, you should take advantage of it. Utilize the other two URLs by linking to specific products or services, a special landing page for those coming from LinkedIn Companies Pages, or your LinkedIn pages for your specific company or a group you've created. Be creative when determining where to link, but make use of this available real estate.

Twitter

Twitter integration is becoming increasingly popular on professional LinkedIn profiles. If you are tweeting on behalf of your company, you should add it to your LinkedIn profile. If you personally tweet in a way that is branded and aligned with your LinkedIn presence, you may want to integrate that Twitter account as well. However, if you use Twitter to keep in touch with friends and family, there is no reason to add it to your LinkedIn profile from an SMO perspective.

The current LinkedIn/Twitter integration allows users to either automatically populate their status updates with every tweet or only those with a pound sign and "in" (#in) added to them. For SMO purposes, you need to control those tweets you want to share with your LinkedIn audience and leave personal tweets out, so it is highly recommended that only those tweets with the company's professional branding that have the potential to drive traffic to a website or another social media property be featured in the status update.

Status Updates

To maximize the status update on LinkedIn for SMO purposes, you should only share information that is relevant, drives website traffic, and is controlled in frequency. Many people automate tweets into their status updates, but LinkedIn is not Twitter. Furthermore, automated tweeting and using the #in solution are not ideal because the status update is not limited to 140 characters, you can select the photos to display, and you can edit the title and description of the post should you wish to do so. I recommend using status updates strategically once or twice a day at most, and manually updating them on LinkedIn so you can make use of the character count, image display, and editing functions. This allows you to create an update in which others might actively engage.

LinkedIn Groups

Your LinkedIn Group

Whether or not you contribute your company's website content to your own LinkedIn Group should be based upon how relevant it is for the community of LinkedIn professionals you have fostered in this space. If your content is truly valuable—which it should be as part of a comprehensive social media marketing strategy—you can contribute your content to spark engagement and initiate discussions within your group. Pay attention to frequency of posting, however, because if you are the only one submitting content and it is always from your own company's website, group members might not stick around.

As mentioned in Chapter 6, the announcement feature should only be reserved for calls to action, but if you are trying to drive traffic back to your website for a special campaign, event, or service that is both relevant to your audience and provides a unique experience such as a discount or value-added extras for fellow LinkedIn Group members, you might want to experiment with this. Just remember that social media is created for people, and any sales messages may backfire.

Other LinkedIn Groups

Another SMO strategy for utilizing LinkedIn Groups is to post your company's website content as a discussion piece in relevant LinkedIn Groups in which you are a member. However, many group members, and especially group managers, may consider personal promotion of website content in the group as link-building spam. For this reason, you always have to submit content that adheres to these three guidelines:

- Your content and posting links are in accordance with the group rules. Every group has different rules, so it is essential that you confirm what they are for every group in which you'd like to post your website content.
- If the group manager contacts you about the content, be able to explain why the content is both relevant to the group and non-self-promotional.
- It is done at a frequency that is not alarming to other LinkedIn Group members. In my previous LinkedIn book, I talked about the importance of the Japanese term "kuuki wo yomu," which literally means, "reading the atmosphere." You don't want to be seen as a self-promotional link spammer, so get a feel for how often people are posting content, and contribute at a pace that is consistent with the current atmosphere of the group.

Some groups welcome outside content because it provides value to group members and provides an opportunity for participation in community discussions. However, group managers can delete and block users from their groups if they feel they are too self-promotional. Each LinkedIn Group experience is different, but introducing your website content to a large audience relevant to your company's products and services makes LinkedIn Groups one of the most attractive places to generate website traffic if done right.

LinkedIn Companies

As mentioned in Chapter 5 regarding LinkedIn Companies, ensure that these pages are optimized by adding the following links:

* Website URL
* Twitter URL
* RSS feed
* Product/service page URL for every service or product
* LinkedIn landing page for every service or product
* YouTube video for every service or product

Applications

Applications have not been extensively covered in this book because they are merely optional components that sales and marketing professionals can use for maximizing LinkedIn for business purposes. Some professional applications exist for niche businesses such as lawyers and legal firms (Lawyer Ratings and Legal Updates), creative agencies (Portfolio Display), and real estate professionals (Real Estate Pro), but there are others that can be utilized for any industry.

WordPress or Blog Link

In addition to posting your blog content in the sections previously mentioned, you can display your most recent blog posts on your profile in a separate, devoted section utilizing either of the following applications:

WordPress is the better of the two applications in terms of look and feel, but your company blog must utilize the WordPress content management system (CMS).

Blog Link works with any blogging CMS. It simply displays the links from the RSS feeds for the three websites listed on your profile. It works seamlessly, but if you list a non-blog URL as one of your websites, such as a Facebook Fan Page, those feeds will be mixed together with your blog feeds in this application.

Google Presentation or SlideShare Presentations

These two applications allow you to display presentations and/or YouTube videos within your profile. If your company has a standard slide deck, corporate video presentation, or product demo you want to promote, utilize one of these two applications.

SlideShare is a social networking site created to share PowerPoint presentations, which can also be utilized for B2B social media marketing. With that in mind, if you plan to post a presentation to your LinkedIn profile, using the SlideShare application allows you to promote your social media presence simultaneously both within LinkedIn and on SlideShare. You can also display YouTube videos through either the SlideShare Presentations or Google Presentation applications. Though video is an extremely powerful medium, it should be used with caution on LinkedIn. The site does not have many interactive features, so a video that is set to automatically play when someone views your prolife profile can seem abrupt. However, should you have a video that is both resourceful and relevant to your target audience, displaying it in your profile using one of these two applications is a powerful way to present content to your potential customers.

Events

Social media can help market your events and generate buzz before, during, and after through the specific use of Twitter and hashtags. LinkedIn also has its own events application that you should use as part of your company's event marketing efforts. It is easy to share the link with your

LinkedIn connections from within the application, the event is indexed by search engines, and every RSVP from the application goes out in the network updates to that person's connections, potentially providing free viral advertising to raise awareness and drive attendance.

Polls

Many companies are turning to polls as an engagement vehicle in social media marketing strategies and to gather market feedback for research purposes. There are many ways to implement polls across multiple social media channels, often using a web-based application such as PollDaddy[56] or Twtpoll,[57] which provide widgets that can be embedded on your website (PollDaddy also includes a Facebook application for your page). If the target audience you want to poll is on LinkedIn, consider creating your next poll using the polls application, which also allows the poll to be embedded on your own website as well as in a Facebook tab using iframe.

The name and headline of the individual who created the poll are displayed, which can help raise awareness about your company, especially if the question and answers are extremely relevant and compelling to your target audience. More importantly, by displaying this poll on your website, you may be able to draw more traffic to LinkedIn, where visitors might end up "bouncing" from your website without a conversion. At this point, you can make a "soft" conversion on LinkedIn by connecting with the person who answered the poll or potentially even began following your company. You can also alert your Facebook fans and Twitter followers of your LinkedIn presence, especially if you comment under the poll in a way that drives them to vote in the poll and engage in the comments.

Integrating Your LinkedIn Presence with Your Website

While it might be counterintuitive with regard to SMO, integrating your LinkedIn presence with your own website allows website visitors to engage

---

56. http://polldaddy.com/
57. http://twtpoll.com/

with you on LinkedIn. The example from the section above about using polls to turn website visitors into soft conversions on LinkedIn is one way to do this. For this reason, you should consider making the following website enhancements to maximize your LinkedIn marketing efforts:

Implement a LinkedIn Share Button on Your Blog

Most companies will implement Facebook like/share and Twitter retweet buttons, but they should embed a button that allows users to share content on LinkedIn as well. Embedding this option on every blog post your company has is a way to encourage blog readers to share your content with their network, and can only work to your advantage. Should you have a WordPress blog, there are many "all-in-one" social sharing plugins that already support the LinkedIn share button. You can also create your own share button on the LinkedIn Developers Page58 and implement it yourself.

Display a Follow Company Badge

The more followers your company has, the greater the chance people will engage with your LinkedIn Companies Page. Furthermore, since there are ways of selecting how many followers a company has when doing a companies search, the number of followers *might* have a role in the default relevance filter for a companies search. After all, the number of followers is one sign of credibility.

LinkedIn offers a follow company badge that can be displayed on your website and lead visitors directly to your LinkedIn Companies Page. The code can be copied and pasted directly from the overview tab on the bottom right-hand side of your company's page.

Display a Company Recommendations Badge

Similar to the share button, this can be created on the LinkedIn Developers Page. The more recommendations for your products and services you can get the better, so consider displaying this on your website to encourage

---

58. http://developer.linkedin.com/community/plugins

more visitors to recommend your company on LinkedIn without leaving your website.

Promote Your LinkedIn Group

While LinkedIn does not provide a standard widget to promote your LinkedIn Group, you can create your own and lead website visitors to your LinkedIn community. This invites interested parties to engage in an active and controlled environment. Simply display your group logo on your website with a link attached to it that leads website visitors directly to your LinkedIn Group.

Paid Media on LinkedIn: Investing in LinkedIn Ads

CHAPTER OBJECTIVES

■ *Learn how to create and appropriately target LinkedIn Ads*
■ *Understand micro-targeting options in depth*

INTENTIONALLY INCLUDED THIS CHAPTER AT THE END OF THE BOOK, rather than the beginning, to show you how many different ways you can develop business and market your company on LinkedIn through the sheer sweat equity of your own efforts. You don't have to "pay to play," and the whole premise of social media marketing is that you receive "earned media" through your own content and engagement efforts. LinkedIn offers those who work in sales, marketing, and business development countless opportunities to generate potential client interest and establish new business relationships at no cost, but it's worth noting that LinkedIn does have a social advertising platform that allows for micro-targeting of specific demographics, similar to what is available on Facebook.

If your company has a large advertising budget that is 100 percent invested in PPC search engine ads, it may make sense to experiment with

LinkedIn ads to test click-through rates (CTR) as well as conversions in comparison to other Internet advertising platforms. The advantage of advertising on LinkedIn is its wealthy and influential user base. According to LinkedIn,[59] the site's ads give you the ability to target:

- 7.9 million business decision makers
- 5.5 million high tech managers
- 4.2 million corporate executives
- 1.3 million small-business owners

It might also make sense to utilize LinkedIn Ads because not every LinkedIn user is active on the site's public forums. Furthermore, there are many users who keep small, tight networks that are difficult to penetrate using the other methods described in this book. For this reason, even though ads might seem counterintuitive to social media marketing, they may be effective for marketing your business.

There are two types of ads on LinkedIn: traditional skyscraper or box display ads, and ads with a bold headline, a small image, and some text description. To buy a traditional display ad on LinkedIn, you need to contact LinkedIn's sales team (and presumably also have a reasonably sized budget), but the headline/image/description ad can be created directly on the LinkedIn Ads section of the website.

This chapter examines how to create these text ads, which are noted with an "Ads by LinkedIn Members" link and appear primarily at the right-hand side or bottom of the following areas of LinkedIn[60] as well as on partner sites that use the same LinkedIn user data called the LinkedIn Audience Network:[61]

- User Profile Pages
- Home Page
- Inbox

59. https://www.linkedin.com/ads/start?src=en-all-ad-li-whats_this
60. http://wind.mn/lianswers3
61. http://wind.mn/lianswers4

- Search Results Pages
- Groups

It should be noted that for PPC ads, LinkedIn might also delete the image from your ad and display the text at the top of the LinkedIn.com homepage.

Getting Started Is Easy

If you've ever been intimidated by using an online ad platform, you will be happy to know that LinkedIn Ads is easy to use and does not require any technical skills. Here are the basic steps on how to create an ad for LinkedIn:

1. Click on the "advertising" link at the bottom of any LinkedIn page or from the home dropdown menu in the top navigation bar. Once you have created an ad, there will be a "Go to LinkedIn Ads >>" link just to the right of the LinkedIn logo that appears at the top left-hand corner of every page. LinkedIn also conveniently places an ads shortcut in the top navigation bar under "home." These immediately lead you to a dashboard that allows for the creation and monitoring of all of your ad campaigns.

2. Once you choose to create an ad, you will enter the "Create Your Ad Campaign" screen, which is where you customize your ad with the following fields:
   - Ad Campaign Name—used for your internal administrative purposes.
   - Ad Destination—in addition to linking to a landing page on your current website, you can also send visitors directly to any part of your LinkedIn Companies Page. The destination of the ad should be customized for the demographic targeted.
   - Ad Details—this is where you enter the main components of the ad: an image (which will be resized to fit a 50x50 square), a 25-character headline, and a 75-character description.

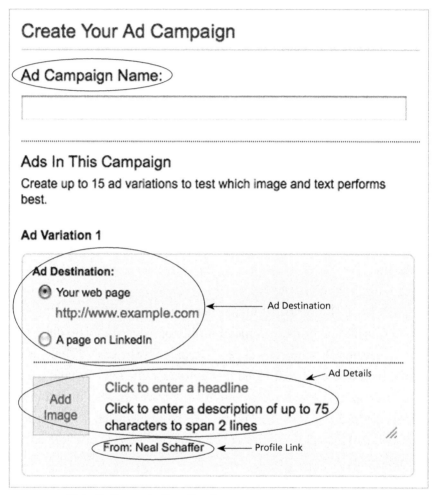

FIGURE 9.1   *LinkedIn Companies Page Creation*

- Profile Link—the bottom of the Ad Details will display "From:" and provide you with the opportunity to display your "Profile Link," which is a link to either your profile or company page. Click on this area to toggle the choices. Needless to say, this provides extra credibility should you decide to use a link here other than "Other" which leads users to one of your LinkedIn assets instead of an external website.
- Add a Variation—LinkedIn Ads allows you to create up to 15 variations of an ad so you can properly test which ad image and text combination performs best. Creating a variation is optional.

That's it! Once you select "next step," you are ready to start micro-targeting your ad.

Micro-Targeting Options

Advertising on a social platform such as LinkedIn allows marketers to micro-target specific demographics to a degree that isn't possible using traditional Internet ad platforms such as Google AdSense. LinkedIn's demographic is ideal for sales, marketing, and business development professionals, and its ad platform delivers on the promise of allowing marketers to target specific user groups in a variety of ways.

LinkedIn made a significant change to its previous ad platform, LinkedIn DirectAds, and renamed it early in 2011.[62] If you have used LinkedIn DirectAds and didn't like the targeting options, it is worth reintroducing yourself to its advertising platform. LinkedIn used to limit the number of potential targeting categories, but the current platform allows users to fine-tune choices from as many of the several demographic categories as they wish:

GEOGRAPHY

You can choose up to ten locations, which are defined as continents, countries, cities, and metropolitan areas for large cities. Whether you need local, national, or international coverage, LinkedIn provides the ability to target your audience in the locations where many LinkedIn users live and conduct business. When compared with Google AdWords, selection options are fewer, but at least marketers have the ability to conveniently target specific geographic regions.

COMPANY

LinkedIn Ads allows you to target ads to current employees of the companies selected here. When you enter the company name, LinkedIn scours the LinkedIn Companies database and returns the closest matching selection

---

62. http://wind.mn/wsjliads

as well as ten similar companies you might consider targeting. If you do not want to target by company but rather by industry, you can do this by selecting "categories of companies" and choosing up to ten industries that mimic the industries displayed in the LinkedIn Companies database. This allows for strategic targeting of markets you'd like to specifically penetrate and the flexibility to reach a wider audience should you prefer to create broad visibility across several industries.

JOB TITLE

The ability to target by current job tile of LinkedIn users allows for ease in reaching those who might be interested in buying or using a particular product or service. One potential issue with this option, however, is that those known under one job title at a certain company might be called something different at another company. To account for this variance, LinkedIn Ads displays ten similar titles that are close to the original title you suggested. For instance, choosing "chief marketing officer" will display titles such as vice president marketing, senior vice president marketing, and executive vice president marketing.

If you want to target users with a broader selection of job titles, you can choose categories of job titles, which consist of job function as well as seniority. The problem with these selections is that they are not based on user-generated content. For instance, whereas the job title option targets users who list that particular title as their current title, the job functions selection includes concepts such as "entrepreneur," and it is difficult to determine how LinkedIn determines who qualifies when there is no option to select these functions on the user profile. The seniority selections are a bit more precise in that titles such as manager and director can be detected directly from the titles LinkedIn users themselves entered in their user profiles. For the best results, you might want to stick with the specific job titles option so you know you are indeed targeting the intended audience.

GROUP

The ability to target LinkedIn users who are members of specific groups is fascinating. On the one hand, you can directly engage with most users of a group simply by joining the group and sending a message. On the other hand, users can only join up to 50 groups, and there might be groups run by competitors that you cannot access. In such cases, it is possible to target these audiences with a LinkedIn Ads campaign. In general, those that join groups can be considered more "active" on LinkedIn and thus potentially more prone to act on a LinkedIn ad.

GENDER AND AGE

You can target gender as well as age, though the age groups are very broad (18-24, 25-34, 35-54, and 55+). Though not generally an important market indicator, selecting appropriate age groups at least helps better ensure that those in unintended age groups don't potentially click your ads.

LINKEDIN AUDIENCE NETWORK

As noted, you can target the LinkedIn Audience Network with your ads. Theoretically, you can only target those users who log in to third-party sites using their LinkedIn credentials, so in order to reach the broadest base of LinkedIn users, it doesn't make sense to place your ad in the audience network. However, should LinkedIn decide to allow for refined selection and add an analytics feature, similar to what Google AdWords offers for control of which your sites your ads will be displayed in, it may be worth revisiting and considering.

The approximate number of LinkedIn users you potentially target with your current options is displayed in the top right-hand corner of the screen, helping you determine if you've targeted enough potential users or if you need to narrow your focus to a smaller demographic. Though social media marketing is about earned media and engagement, if you already have a PPC budget, you should try experimenting and confirming the ROI of LinkedIn ads for yourself.

Determining Your LinkedIn Ads Budget

If you have followed the above instructions, after selecting your targeted options you will proceed to a screen where you need to choose between

CASE STUDY

Using LinkedIn Ads to Generate Business

I mentioned Rypple's success with its company page previously in this book. In addition to its use of LinkedIn's Companies Pages, the company also has experience using LinkedIn Ads that is worth noting. Despite how active Rypple is throughout LinkedIn, there are always some potential customers that can't be reached, and in those cases, LinkedIn Ads is the ideal platform to utilize. Decision makers at Rypple like how LinkedIn's platform is evolving, and they believe these changes will result in more of their target customers becoming more active on LinkedIn.

BACKGROUND

Marketers at Rypple had traditionally invested in pay-per-click (PPC) campaigns using Google AdWords. They began experimenting with the LinkedIn Ads platform to learn how effective it could be at reaching people within the company's target demographic.

WHAT HAPPENED

After some experimentation, they realized that, with LinkedIn Ads, the CPC as well as the cost-per-lead (CPL) were higher than comparative campaigns on Google AdWords. Through experiments with different types of ads and targets in various campaigns on and off for twelve months, they realized the leads they obtained through LinkedIn were generally more expensive but also more qualified. This led to better working opportunities and a better chance of closing business compared with campaigns on other platforms. In essence, the company chose quality over quantity.

SUMMARY

Because this was a PPC campaign, it took time and money for staff at Rypple to figure out which marketing options worked better than others. They primarily used the role, company, and industry categories to target audiences on LinkedIn, and they recently found success targeting the role of "internal leaders"—people who are most likely to become Rypple's customers. Based on this strategy, they drove a lot more interest and qualified leads which, if closed as predicted, will take their cumulative LinkedIn Ads campaign from the initial investment to a positive ROI in the near future. They are confident that, with proper targeting, LinkedIn Ads will be a smart investment of their marketing budget well into the future.

Pay Per Click (CPC) and Pay Per 1,000 Impressions (CPM), both with minimum bids of $2.00. This area also shows a suggested bid range, a daily budget (with a minimum of $10), and an option to run the ad continuously or end on a specific date.

In order to choose the right CPC or CPM, maximum bid, and daily budget, you will need to experiment with different combinations of these options as well as with your targeted audience to find the best overall ROI of your LinkedIn Ads campaign. Because the ROI of an online ad campaign can be clearly tracked through web analytics with a crisply designed landing page and call to action, the first thing you need to do is set a budget for your campaign. If you already have a budget for search engine marketing or currently run social ads on Facebook, begin by moving one percent of that budget to LinkedIn for a glimpse of the potential ROI of social ads on that site as well.

In determining your LinkedIn Ads budget, consider how much a lead or closed deal is worth. If decision makers for your product or service are included in the LinkedIn demographic, and you can advertise for a few dollars per click for a product or service that is worth tens or hundreds of times that amount, it makes sense to include LinkedIn Ads in your marketing mix.

You can track the efficiency of your ads by clicking on the reporting tab, which appears on the LinkedIn Ads dashboard that you gain access to once you schedule the first ad. Downloadable reports by campaign or ad performance by day provide key performance metrics from which you can calculate the ROI of your ads. This provides data that allows for refinement of ad campaigns for the most effective targeting options.

Pay to Play?

WHEN YOU FIRST BEGIN USING LINKEDIN, YOU WILL MORE than likely sign up for the site's standard free account. This free service is what most people use, and it is sufficient for those who simply want to begin the networking process. With the free account, you can set up a profile; join, participate in, and create groups; and ask and answer questions, so there certainly is value in utilizing what LinkedIn offers at no cost.

In "Windmill Networking: Maximizing LinkedIn," everything I wrote was related to the free account on LinkedIn, and I truly believe there are only a few people who need to bump their subscriptions up so they can take advantage of the paid services available on the site. Recruiters, for example, should take advantage of the site for its advanced search filter functionalities as well as the LinkedIn platform designed specifically for those working in the recruitment industry, which is called LinkedIn Talent Advantage.

LinkedIn recently changed its business model for paid accounts by allowing users with free accounts to purchase InMails à la carte for $10 apiece.[63] Gaining access to InMails was one of the primary reasons for having a paid account, so some people may be wondering why the company would encourage people to buy InMails instead of purchasing a paid subscription. However, in tandem with this change, LinkedIn also lowered the price of the Business account, which includes three InMails a month, to $19.95 a month as part of an annual subscription. In other words, if you find yourself realizing the value of InMails and are sending at least two a month, it is cheaper to simply buy the Business subscription. LinkedIn also offers a Personal Plus account for less than $10 a month, which isn't found through a direct URL but can be accessed following the directions on the next page. As with everything on LinkedIn, upgrading to certain accounts will make more sense for some professionals than others.

Exploring the Benefits of a Paid Account: LinkedIn Personal Plus

In addition to recruiters who might pay to use certain features on LinkedIn, there are also features available through premium subscriptions that would be of great advantage to sales professionals. First and foremost, a paid account allows those in sales to save a lot of time during the prospecting process. If you're looking for specific types of people in specific organizations, these accounts let users vet more search results, which allows them to quickly find those potential customers for whom they're looking. Until the writing of this book, I would have advised sales professionals to consider the advertised paid version of LinkedIn because it also provides access to InMail, which, as I stated in Chapter 4, is the "Hail Mary" of connecting with a specific person when you have no other way

---

63. https://www.linkedin.com/secure/inmail_v4?displayProducts=

to do so. However, as mentioned earlier, LinkedIn's recent policy change means that users don't have to pay for premium accounts to take advantage of this feature anymore.

That said, people working in a B2B environment will most likely be using LinkedIn more than other social media outlets to reach out to potential customers, create buzz about their products and services, and establish company credibility. If you are dedicated to using LinkedIn for developing your business prospects and are on the site nearly every day, you should consider upgrading to a paid account.

Before you begin shopping around through LinkedIn's paid platform options, you should know that the platform I initially recommend for sales and marketing professionals because of its inexpensive price is not publicly advertised. This platform, called LinkedIn Personal Plus, is a package option that was available long before the current packages and costs less than the current advertised packages, but at the time of writing this book it is still available for purchase. To access the Personal Plus option, please try the following method, which one of my readers directly confirmed with LinkedIn Customer Service:

1. From your home page of LinkedIn, navigate to the box on the right-hand side that says "Who's viewed your profile?" and click through to the next page.
2. In the lower right-hand side of this page, there is a widget for Profile Stats Pro. Click on the button that says, "upgrade now."
3. The next page offers the menu of paid platforms publicly displayed on LinkedIn as well as LinkedIn Personal Plus, which can only be found using this path through the site.

LinkedIn Personal Plus offers a more thorough offering of services than free subscribers receive though a less robust selection than the advertised paid options of Business and Business Plus accounts. For $9.95 per month (or $7.95 per month if you sign up for an annual subscription), you get the following features through LinkedIn Personal Plus:

The Profile Organizer

This feature allows users to save profiles into virtual folders as detailed in Chapter 9. As a business professional, you likely don't have the extra time to print out the profiles of potential customers and clients, but the Profile Organizer offers a quick and easy way to organize your professional and networking contacts as well as those with whom you'd like to get in touch into virtual folders, regardless if they are a first-degree connection or not. You will be given five folders in which to save these profiles.

Five additional introductions

With a free LinkedIn account, you get five free introductions. The LinkedIn Personal Plus platform gives you five more free introductions. Though this feature isn't necessarily valuable given the fact you can find other ways to introduce yourself, it is a part of the package.

The opportunity to join the OpenLink network

As a member of this network, a small logo appears next to your name throughout LinkedIn. This is a way to tell others that you welcome the opportunity to communicate with them and are available for open networking. As a result, this feature also allows you to opt in to the OpenLink message functionality, which means that people who visit your profile can send you a message regardless of their connectivity status to you. If your goal is to be as approachable as possible on LinkedIn, this is the feature that best allows for you to achieve that goal. As a sales and marketing professional, the opportunities that can result from the OpenLink network may potentially be worth the purchase price of LinkedIn Personal Plus.

Profile Stats Pro

This collection of analytics provides information about your profile. For example, you can see the complete list of who has viewed your profile, where those people came from, how many people have viewed your profile, and the keywords that led them to your profile. Seeing the complete list of those who viewed your profile can spark engagement with a potential customer if they visited your profile but never contacted you for whatever reason. Of course, this assumes that the visitor is using the feature that displays their full profile name when they browse other profiles. The analytics feature has questionable value for the data it provides, but if you're particularly interested in how well your keywords are working in search results, this might be helpful information.

Other features

When you purchase LinkedIn Personal Plus, you also have access to a few other features that you may find helpful. You have the ability to automate your search results with three saved search alerts per week as well as view the first names of your third-degree connections. None of these features alone are the selling points for this paid platform, but they might be a nice side bonus.

Business and Business Plus Paid Accounts

If you see the value in the Personal Plus account, you might also find it more advantageous to choose the Business account at the onset instead. For only a slightly higher price, you get access to all the features in the Personal Plus account as well as these additional features:

- Three InMails, which in itself more than pays for the investment
- The ability to see 300 search results at once instead of 100, which could improve your efficiency if you are often using the LinkedIn advanced people search
- Access to four Premium Search Filters to help you better and more quickly find the person you are searching for. These filters are seniority, company size, interests, and Fortune (1000) status
- Five saved search results instead of three
- Five additional free introductions, which gives you 15 to use at any time

Features	Your Current Account **Personal Plus**	Recommended **Business** ⊙ Annual: $19.95/month* ○ Monthly: $24.95/month Upgrade	**Business Plus** ○ Annual: $39.95/month* ○ Monthly: $49.95/month Upgrade
Contact anyone directly with InMail -- Response Guaranteed!		3 ($30 value)	10 ($100 value)
See more profiles when you search	100	300	500
Zero in on profiles with Premium Search Filters		Premium Filters	Premium Filters
See expanded profiles of everyone on LinkedIn		Yes	Yes
Who's Viewed My Profile: Get the full list	Yes	Yes	Yes
Save important profiles and notes using Profile Organizer	5 folders	5 folders	25 folders
Automate your search with Saved Search Alerts	3 per week	5 per week	7 per week
Get introduced to the companies you're targeting	10 outstanding	15 outstanding	25 outstanding
See names of your 3rd degree and Group connections	First Name	First Name	First Name
Get the real story on anyone with Reference Search	Yes	Yes	Yes
Let anyone message you for free with OpenLink	Yes	Yes	Yes
Get Priority Customer Service	Yes	Yes	Yes
Show less... ▲			

FIGURE 13.1   *Comparing LinkedIn Paid Accounts*

For about double the price of the Business plan, LinkedIn also provides a Business Plus account with the following additional benefits in addition to those offered with the Business subscription plan:

- Ten InMails; you would pay $40 per month as part of an annual subscription plan, and that means that you'd essentially be getting ten InMails for the price of four in addition to all of the other benefits this account provides
- 500 profiles per search result
- 25 Profile Organizer virtual folders
- Seven saved search alerts per week
- 25 introductions

The key benefits to any paid membership are the ability to join the OpenLink network, gain access to the Profile Organizer, and using Profile Stats Pro to engage with someone who might have left a virtual footprint on your profile. However, if you spend a lot of time doing searches and regularly sending InMails, you will definitely want to upgrade to a Business or even Business Plus account, which should be determined by how many InMails you normally send.

Your Daily LinkedIn Routine and ROI

CHAPTER OBJECTIVES

- *Learn how sales and marketing professionals can effectively manage their time on LinkedIn*
- *Devise a timesaving strategy for managing a company's presence on LinkedIn*
- *Determine your own ROI metrics so you know that you and everyone at your company is optimizing time spent on LinkedIn for maximum efficiency*

B Y NOW YOU SHOULD BE FEELING CONFIDENT ABOUT THE POWER of LinkedIn as a unique and compelling social networking tool for sales and marketing professionals. Although there is a lot built into the site, you should be better able to navigate through its functionalities while maximizing those components that best suit your business' needs.

If you're like most professionals, though, the issue isn't convincing yourself that social media in general and LinkedIn specifically are important tools for networking, meeting and exceeding your business goals, and closing deals. Rather, the problem is that doing all of these things—managing a LinkedIn Companies Page, facilitating a group, asking and answering questions and answers—can take up a lot of valuable time.

The key to capitalizing on the business capabilities of LinkedIn (and all social media for that matter) is to create a daily routine where you can efficiently and effectively have an optimal presence. With the right routine, you should be able to continuously market your company and potentially develop business through online connections with potentially only a few minutes of time every day.

A successful company will spend time on LinkedIn and other forms of social media, but it is important to realize that these websites do not exist in a vacuum. Business owners should still be employing the traditional sales and marketing techniques that work for their particular company in their particular niche and geographic region. At the end of the day, your company still needs to focus on its ROI; everything it does on LinkedIn— as well as the results of those activities—should tie back to its core purpose for integrating its sales and marketing efforts in social media. Creating a LinkedIn routine and monitoring how much time you spend on it each day will help you decide if the time devoted to the site is equal to the ROI you get as a result.

Any social media business book must have some mention of ROI, but because there are so many different objectives that companies and professionals have for being on social media websites and thus so many varying metrics that could be used to measure their success, I want to mention my own definition of social media ROI, which my clients and company have been employing successfully. Having a daily routine definitely helps to measure that ROI.

The Daily Routine: Professional Perspective

Sales and marketing professionals will need to spend some time each day using their personal profiles to interact with others on LinkedIn. There's no need to revisit the actual profile creation on a frequent basis, so the key to maintain mindshare with your network is to take the time to log in to LinkedIn at least once a week and ideally every workday if possible to stay in touch with your connections. Providing a new status update, asking a question, or starting a new discussion are all legitimate ways to stay in your network's feed. This lets all of your connections know that you are active and within reach, and it keeps your name fresh in their minds. While you're on the site, scroll through your network updates and see if there are any opportunities to reach out, connect with, or help people in your network. Doing any of these tasks should take no more than five or ten minutes.

Individual engagement with those outside of your first-degree connections revolves primarily around joining, monitoring, and participating in relevant groups. When you sign up for a group, you can choose to opt in to receive a daily or weekly digest of group activities, and it is always in a professional's best interest to choose the daily option. This daily digest is delivered directly to the email inbox and allows for easy monitoring of any discussions or questions in which engagement with potential clients or stakeholders is feasible, thus resulting in possible new business in the future. If there is a marketing assistant who can monitor this process and notify you when there is an opportunity for engagement, consider delegating this task to him or her.

In addition to monitoring your groups, it's important to keep an eye on the LinkedIn Answers feature and figure out which category you should own. Consider subscribing to the RSS feed for this task to determine questions and answers that require your input, and, again, employ the services of someone else in order to cut down on the time you personally spend on this daily task if possible.

If you want to invest more of your time on LinkedIn, that effort should be focused on conducting research for potential business by looking for and connecting with prospective clients or engaging in more discussions in more groups. This, of course, could take several hours a day, so the amount of time spent on this task should be based on how much you are using LinkedIn as a part of your sales and marketing efforts.

The Daily Routine: Corporate Perspective

In any B2B social media situation, regardless of whether you're using LinkedIn or some other networking site, your company's online relevancy and mindshare are a direct result of both engaging with your potential customer to fill the funnel as well as creating and curating original and third-party content and then sharing it with others as an important part of the engagement process. Therefore, from a corporate point of view, managing content is one of the most important aspects of the daily routine. Every day, determine whether you have any new internal content to share with members of your corporate group or in any industry-related groups on which your company or marketing team has a strong presence. Even if you don't have any original content, do a search for relevant material from a non-competing third-party that fellow group members might find interesting and worthwhile. Frequent postings from a corporate perspective help ensure your business maintains mindshare with those with whom you interact in the LinkedIn community, even if that content doesn't originate from your own website.

It's not enough just to post new content, however. In order to maximize your presence on LinkedIn, you have to engage with interested parties. There isn't much that can be done on your company's page, so time is probably best spent in the groups you own. As a community manager, you should spend some time every day monitoring the group, responding to comments and discussions, starting new discussions, and otherwise ensuring that the group remains active and interesting for current members and entices new members to join. Spend the time necessary to ensure these things are happening, which, in turn, should increase your influence and gain mindshare in the online business sphere. In addition, make it a habit to frequently ask your sales team if there are any activities you can do on LinkedIn to better align your company to help them meet their targets.

Determining the ROI of Your LinkedIn Efforts

You have an objective for buying this book and being active on LinkedIn using the methods and strategies discussed herein. I hope you now also have a daily LinkedIn routine that governs the tactics you will employ on a daily basis to help you reach your objective; ideally that objective is also aligned with your corporate social media strategy. In simple terms, the ROI of your LinkedIn activities are governed by whether or not you reached your objective. There are various objectives that sales and marketing professionals might have, and potential metrics to measure your LinkedIn efforts could include:

- Attaining x number of leads per day/week/month on LinkedIn
- Utilizing LinkedIn to help close x deals per day/week/month
- Achieving group membership of x members
- Increasing company page followers to x people
- Increasing product/service recommendations by x clients
- Increasing the amount of web traffic originating from LinkedIn
- Increasing the conversion rate of web traffic originating from LinkedIn
- Increasing the conversion rate of your LinkedIn landing pages
- ROI of your PPC advertising

Armed with a distinct objective, LinkedIn routine, and measurable metrics, you can now begin to track the ROI of your LinkedIn activities on a weekly, monthly, or quarterly basis. One important thing to note is that, with the exception of PPC advertising, the difficulty in calculating social media ROI is that social media is free, but time spent is not, and that needs to be considered. If you can crisply define your LinkedIn routine and limit it to 5, 15, or even 30 minutes a day, you can then compare it to the metrics you created to determine whether or not you are meeting your objectives.

Another thing to note is, as with any other social media activity, there are numerous intangible benefits from your efforts on LinkedIn that can't be defined by a metric. They include important aspects of marketing such as offline word of mouth, goodwill, and mindshare.

If you are meeting or exceeding your objectives with your current daily routine, consider increasing your investment of time and decreasing time and/or money spent elsewhere.

If you are not meeting your objectives then something is wrong with your daily LinkedIn routine. Are you doing the right things on the site, or is there a way to improve on your actions? Are you spending your time in the right areas of LinkedIn targeting the right type of users? Consider tweaking your actions and experiment with different ways to increase your ROI. Your metric objectives may have been unrealistic when you started, but as you continue to tweak your LinkedIn activities and improve your ROI, keep working toward your objectives, however lofty they might seem.

While many are confused about the ROI of their social media efforts and complain about the lack of tools from which to measure it, using a holistic approach as recommended above will give you an excellent feel over time as to the fruits of your efforts on LinkedIn.

Appendix A: Resources to Help You Stay Up to Date

OCIAL MEDIA AND ONLINE NETWORKING HAVE BECOME A MUCH bigger part of our corporate culture and the way we do business in recent years, and the amount of literature available on the subject is practically incomprehensible. It's certainly a good idea to follow social media trends in order to maximize the reach of your online presence and connections, but trying to follow and read everything is impossible, so I'd like to offer some resources that I recommend are worth your time.

This diverse array of resources offers not only a basic coverage of LinkedIn and other social media networking websites but also highlights the very best when it comes to breaking ground in social media news and providing information on new and changing technologies.

Please note that, except for the Windmill Networking materials, I am not personally affiliated with any of these third-person blogs, websites, or books. I have not been asked to endorse them, nor am I being paid to promote them. Rather, I have found these resources to be the ones I turn to for information on social media and networking in the digital age.

Websites

Windmill Networking

http://windmillnetworking.com/

Social media is an evolving tool, and what is new and fresh today might be out of date tomorrow. New features to LinkedIn may revolutionize the way we connect with each other, but even small changes and additions can change the way we maximize our usage of the site. Though this book was accurate at the time of writing and publication, chances are there will be changes to LinkedIn before too long, so check out the official Windmill Networking blog for updates on the content in this book as well as information about other social networking sites. The focus of the Windmill Networking blog is on social media strategy for businesses and professionals.

The other way to keep up with my latest blog posts, social media tools, events, and upcoming books is to subscribe to my monthly newsletter at http://wind.mn/windml.

Social Media Today

http://socialmediatoday.com/

This online community for professionals working in public relations, marketing, advertising, and business in general is a source of lively conversation about the tools, platforms, people, and companies that are changing the way we conduct business. Members in the community contribute the content, which is then curated by the staff, which means the site is updated frequently and from several points of view. Note that I am also a contributor to this site.

CustomerThink

http://www.customerthink.com/

This global community consists of business leaders focused on creating profitable customer-centric enterprises. Most topics of discussion on CustomerThink are consumer-facing in focus, including posts on customer relationship management and customer experience management. In addition to frequent posts, visitors will find white papers, reports, and webcasts as well. Note that I am also a contributor to this site.

HubSpot

http://blog.hubspot.com/

As stated on its website, HubSpot is "an all-in-one marketing software platform for small- and medium-sized businesses." In essence, it's a resource tapped by thousands of businesses in order to generate hundreds of thousands of leads for their company needs. HubSpot marketing software offers companies tools for blogging, marketing analytics, content management, social media, and much more. While I am not a user nor endorse HubSpot products and services, this company clearly understands the role that resourceful content plays in social media marketing and offers a plethora of social media resources to the visitor, starting with its marketing blog.

Social Media Examiner

http://www.socialmediaexaminer.com/

The tagline for Social Media Examiner is "Your Guide to the Social Media Jungle," and that's exactly what navigating the online world can feel like at times. With daily content and basic information presented in a simple fashion, this website breaks down social media in an easy-to-understand manner and helps businesses learn how they can best utilize these online tools to find leads, increase sales, and generate brand awareness.

Mashable

http://mashable.com/

Mashable tends to be the go-to site for all things related to social media, technology, and web culture. At its core, Mashable is a news site with reports on breaking web news and reviews on relevant online resources. The site also offers social media resources and guides. If it is related to technology, gadgets, media, design, business, or marketing, chances are you can find information about it on Mashable.

Books

Windmill Networking: Understanding, Leveraging & Maximizing LinkedIn
Neal Schaffer (Author)
http://wind.mn/windbook

My first book is a LinkedIn reference manual that introduces new as well as experienced users to the site and explains the functionalities in comprehensive detail. If you have any additional questions about how certain functions on LinkedIn can be better utilized beyond business-specific purposes, or if you'd like to learn about or refresh your memory on some of the basics of the site, this is the comprehensive reference manual you should turn to for answers.

The Big Book of Social Media: Case Studies, Stories, Perspectives
Robert Fine (Editor), Sam Feist (Foreword)
http://wind.mn/bigsocialbook

Hopefully you're convinced by now that active participation in social media matters and works for business-minded people, but if you still need proof, pick up this book, which details several stories about how social media is changing the world we live in. In full disclosure, I contributed a case study to a chapter in "The Big Book of Social Media" that is not included in this book about how one of my social media strategy consulting clients successfully developed a user community with more than 10,000 members, which has become a prime business development vehicle for them.

Inbound Marketing: Get Found Using Google, Social Media, and Blogs
(New Rules Social Media Series)
Brian Halligan (Author), Dharmesh Shah (Author), David Meerman Scott (Foreword)
http://wind.mn/windbook3

Traditional marketing practices encourage those in sales, marketing, and business development to push their message out to potential customers, but new media channels such as Google and social media are making it easier for those customers to find you. This book is a step-by-step guide to being found through Google, blogs, and on social media sites. It should be noted that the founders of Hubspot wrote this book, and it spawned the term "inbound marketing," which has now become a commonplace term in social media marketing.

Social Media Metrics: How to Measure and Optimize Your Marketing
Investment (New Rules Social Media Series)
Jim Sterne (Author), David Meerman Scott (Foreword)
http://wind.mn/windbook2

If you want to bypass everything that explains why social media is important and how to participate in it, and, instead, focus on how to measure the success of your marketing efforts, this is the book for you. Billed as "the only guide devoted exclusively to social media metrics," this resource offers specific metrics you can use to ensure your marketing efforts and dollars are spent right.

Social Media ROI: Managing and Measuring Social
Media Efforts in Your Organization
Olivier Blanchard (Author)
http://wind.mn/windbook1

This book is a compilation of the best practices for strategy, planning, execution, measurement, analysis, and optimization. "Social Media ROI" is a how-to guide that offers practical solutions for all things related to social media including how to structure programs, attract followers, define metrics, and manage crises. Regardless of your company size, chances are you'll find something of value in this book.

If you're interested in learning more about other books regarding LinkedIn and other social media channels, feel free to browse these top social media book reading lists as well:

Top 15 Recommended Social Media Books of 2010:
http://wind.mn/topsmbooks2010

Top 15 Recommended Social Media Books of 2009:
http://wind.mn/topsmbooks2009

Appendix B:
Additional Case Studies

If you would like your LinkedIn success story to be considered for future publication in this book, please send details to the author directly at neal@ windmillnetworking.com.

CASE STUDY

Reconnecting with Old Contacts Yields Business

How did we manage customer relationships before the digital age? We kept records of our clients, of course, but social media beckons us to get online to continue fostering those relationships we've made in the past. Though we may have lost track of those clients we had prior to the technological leap, LinkedIn offers features—including the ability to search and send invitations to connect—that can help you get back in touch with them. Reestablishing those long-lost relationships utilizing the powerful LinkedIn platform may even result in new business.

BACKGROUND
Ken Miller's building energy code consulting business[1] was established in the 1970s, and over the years, the company has collected data on several thousands of clients. His company conducted business with many of these people prior to the days of online networking, however, and, over time, it has lost touch with several of them. Some of these clients are now with different employers and, in some cases, there isn't even an email address available in the current database with which to contact these former clients.

---

1. http://energycompliance.com/

WHAT HAPPENED

Now that Miller's company has become active and visible on LinkedIn, he has been found by as well as reached out to former clients. Because LinkedIn doesn't require that you know someone's email address to search, Ken has been able to find many people with whom his company did business in the past by going through the entire database his company has kept as well as his personal contact list. When he recognizes former clients on LinkedIn (through first-degree connections), he confirms their statuses on the corporate database and sends invitations to connect. Though this hasn't necessarily led to new business for his company directly from these former clients, it has led him to other referrals through their connections.

Miller also makes it a point to post updates regarding topical issues his company is working on for certain clients without mentioning specific names in order to showcase his firm's experience and the scope of projects on which they are currently working.

SUMMARY

In six months time, Miller's company has closed on four business deals because of LinkedIn—a five percent increase in the number of jobs it would normally have. These deals range in size from a few hundred dollars to several thousand dollars, but they bring in about double what the firm would make from a typical job not contracted through LinkedIn.

CASE STUDY

Asking Questions as an Engagement Vehicle

Sales and business development professionals know that their business is a social venture, but despite being hyper-social offline, many aren't all that social on networking platforms such as LinkedIn, where many of their professional peers spend time. This case study highlights someone who has been extremely social in networking and is referred to as a LION or LinkedIn Open Networker. "Windmill Networking:

Maximizing LinkedIn" goes into more detail about the LinkedIn open networking movement and whether or not to become a LION, but this case study clearly illustrates how actively reaching out to new people online, whether through virtually connecting with your networks or engaging in discussions on online public forums, can lead to similar offline business results.

BACKGROUND

Ian Haines[1] received an invitation to join LinkedIn from someone he had worked with in December 2005. He had never heard of the site, but he joined, put together a basic profile, and began looking through the site to invite people he knew or had done business with in the last 15 years. When Haines realized he could see the job titles of senior executives at certain companies, he reappraised LinkedIn's usefulness as a business tool. In order to get access to these executive employees and people with whom he had once done business, he had to enlarge his connections base in order to establish ways to develop relationships with specific people.

As he scanned through his limited connections, he discovered someone who said he was an open networker and would happily connect to anyone. This person also suggested that in order to increase the number of people you can see on LinkedIn, you have to connect to a super connector.[2] Haines found and connected with a super connector, and then decided that, to build the size and reach of his network, he would become an open networker.[3] As an open networker Haines connects to anyone that asks him to connect; he never hits the "I don't know" button and never discriminates by the seniority of an invite, number of connections someone has, or industry sector. The strategy, he says, is all about who his connections are connected to and to whom their connections are connected.

WHAT HAPPENED

Haines is a member of 50 LinkedIn Groups, nearly all of which are related to his business and industry, and he is also the manager of a group related to his industry sector. As the groups began to build

---

1. http://www.ianmhaines.co.uk/
2. http://wind.mn/lions2011
3. http://windmillnetworking.com/2008/07/11/what-is-a-linkedin-lion/

momentum and develop a decent membership, he became a regular contributor and asked lots of questions. "I have found that the whole point of business networking is being seen by your peers as someone who is important in terms of opinion or expertise within their sector," he said. "When you achieve this status, opportunities start to flow."

In one particular instance, Haines posted a response to a question in a group about sales and marketing platforms and which ones he recommended. The person who asked the question and Haines then engaged in email correspondence and by phone. At the time, he imparted what he knew without any thought as to what it could mean for him, which he says is the very essence and spirit of networking. A few months later, the company for which he answered the question approached him. They required his expertise to manage a major piece of outsourced work on their behalf—a direct extension of the assistance he had given selflessly just a few months prior. "I can't honestly say that you can always give of your time in an unselfish way when asked by just anyone," Haines said, "but usually there are benefits which may come in the form of work, recommendations, or introductions to people who can provide you with work."

SUMMARY

Haines made £72,000 (about US$120,000) over the course of the year from that particular business deal. He spends two or three hours a day on the site and picks up about five serious clients a year from his LinkedIn activities. LinkedIn helps him generate about £300,000 (about US$500,000) per year.

CASE STUDY

The Potential Revenue-Generating Power of Groups Online and in Person

LinkedIn is a powerful online networking tool, and connecting with others through groups is one of its most powerful features. It's important to remember, however, that groups work best through active discussions, interested members, and a give-and-take atmosphere.

When we begin to invest more time in social media, it's easy to forget that there are real people behind each and every one of the profiles we encounter on LinkedIn. Sometimes, however, the most powerful online networking groups have been greatly enhanced through face-to-face promotion.

BACKGROUND

Lisa Hendrickson[1] is the founder and owner of CallThatGirl.biz, a PC/Macintosh computer support helpdesk company located in Minneapolis, Minnesota. Throughout her career, she had been collecting business cards, and one day she sent invitations to connect on LinkedIn to all of those people from whom she had gotten cards. Hendrickson wasn't exactly sure how to capitalize on the relationships she had made with these new connections, however brief their encounters might have been, and it wasn't until she started using social media a bit more aggressively and joined a LinkedIn Group that she realized how she could do so.

In early 2008, Hendrickson searched for local groups on LinkedIn and discovered LinkedMinnesota, a networking and discussion group for all professionals in the state of Minnesota. She joined, saw the potential benefits in growing the community, and spread the word about the group via avid offline networking. The group grew significantly through Hendrickson's actions, and she was eventually offered ownership of the group.

WHAT HAPPENED

As the new owner and manager of the LinkedMinnesota Group, Hendrickson invested time and effort in promoting the group every time she had the opportunity, whether online or in person. Enthusiasm grew within the group and more people joined, excited to take part in the activity. Hendrickson took on volunteer help to assist in developing and managing the group. Together, Hendrickson and these other particularly active members of LinkedMinnesota continued to promote the group's value within LinkedMinnesota discussions, within other LinkedIn Groups, and in real-world networking sessions.

Hendrickson specifically enlisted the help of other entrepreneurs to spread the word about the LinkedIn Group, and she has found that

---

1. http://www.linkedin.com/in/callthatgirl

they are eager to talk up the group at LinkedMinnesota sponsored events. In return, she has rewarded these efforts by giving volunteers website placement and mentions in group announcements every once in awhile.

Today there are nearly 20,000 members in the LinkedMinnesota Group and approximately 700 new people join every month, making it the largest LinkedIn Group dedicated specifically to Minnesota.

SUMMARY

Hendrickson spends about 15 hours a week managing the group, interacting and connecting with members, and ensuring this online area remains an interesting and engaging networking space. Her time and effort on LinkedMinnesota has paid off tremendously. Her company, CallThatGirl.biz, has acquired more than 400 clients from LinkedIn. In return, Hendrickson has earned more than $60,000 through LinkedIn or from referrals directly related to her LinkedIn activities.

CASE STUDY

How I Developed Business on LinkedIn Groups

Sometimes all it takes is one data point from a social engagement to start a domino effect that can lead to business and then referrals for additional business. With so many ways to engage and learn about other professionals on LinkedIn, there are endless possibilities on where and how you can close your next business deal using this site. This is my own personal contribution to this collection of case studies.

BACKGROUND

As I launched my social media strategy consulting business[1] in January 2010, I realized that I needed to be active in LinkedIn Groups where my target customers were. For the first time in a long time, I followed the advice that I highlighted in "Windmill Networking: Maximizing

---

1. http://windmillnetworking.com/social-media-consulting-services/

LinkedIn" regarding looking at your groups on an Excel spreadsheet and aligning them with keywords that are relevant to your business. I realigned my group memberships and started to subscribe to weekly digests of those groups where I felt my target customers frequented and where the discussions were particularly engaging.

WHAT HAPPENED

One day I noticed a particularly active discussion in a group regarding what the ROI of social media was. The discussion generated a few hundred comments, and the last person who had commented called out to all group members to prove to him what the exact ROI of social media was. I was up to the challenge and I thrive in such discussions. However, instead of responding to him with a comment to the discussion, I instead navigated to his profile to get a better feel for who he was. It turned out that he was a marketing consultant who happened to live in the same county in California where I lived. Furthermore, although he only had around 150 connections, one of them happened to be my brother! This particular person was involved in event planning and had connected with my brother because of his work in the wine industry, although the two didn't know each other personally.

I sent him a personalized message offering to meet him over coffee so I could convince him of the ROI of social media just as he had requested.

SUMMARY

We ended up meeting, and he confided in me that he had a client who was looking for social media expertise. Within a week I was introduced to his client and the deal was closed. In addition, this marketing consultant introduced me as a speaker to an event he produced, which resulted in more business for me.

CASE STUDY

Active Participation in LinkedIn Groups Attracts Business

Though we've spent a lot of this book talking about how sales and marketing professionals can actively pursue business deals using LinkedIn, there are several success stories in which the converse has been true. By actively participating in LinkedIn and providing value in group discussions, through network updates, and by answering questions, some professionals find that interested customers come looking for them.

BACKGROUND

Judy B. Margolis,[1] a Toronto, Canada-based professional business writer, editor, and journalist specializing in strategic marketing and B2B communications, has a long history of working in the writing and editing industry. Focusing on business-related projects, her industry niche—brand advocacy, professional and financial service, B2B, and B2C—was also a field of expertise she excelled in personally. Knowing that people in need of her business writing services could be found on LinkedIn, she quickly became a regular on the site.

WHAT HAPPENED

Upon joining LinkedIn, Margolis completed her profile, including a photo, client recommendations, and writing samples demonstrating her skills. She joined the maximum 50 groups and devoted a lot of time to answering questions, both of which allowed her to become more engaged and visible on the site. Through this active participation, people interested in her professional services began approaching her with business opportunities by inviting her to connect or contacting her via email or phone to inquire about fees.

LinkedIn has helped Margolis acquire four international, three U.S.-based, and several local clients, whom she met both online and through networking opportunities that arose as a result of her membership in geographic-specific LinkedIn Groups.

---

1. http://www.linkedin.com/in/judymargolis2009

SUMMARY

Margolis spends about two hours a day on the website, or about 20 percent of her workday. That's a healthy ROI for someone who credits LinkedIn for approximately one-third of her business.

CASE STUDY

The Challenging Third-Degree Connection

When someone is beyond a second-degree connection, it can be difficult to close the gap between you and that person. LinkedIn offers the opportunity to reach out to third-degree connections, however, and even though it may be challenging to get the right introductions to make the needed connections, it can be done...sometimes with resounding success because of the inherent professional nature of the platform and the professionals that can help connect you with others.

BACKGROUND

Lesley S. Bateman,[1] Senior Marketing Strategist at Design4 Marketing, began using LinkedIn when she wanted to reenter the job market after taking time off to raise her children. She reached out to those people with whom she used to work in the event she ever needed to network for future business purposes. After seeing the benefits, she continued to use it once hired by a marketing firm.

WHAT HAPPENED

Bateman's marketing firm wanted to respond to a request for proposal for the state governor's office to promote adoption. Another agency in the state had been awarded the job the previous year, and Lesley knew it was doubtful her firm would win the entire bid, so she reached out to the CEO of the previous year's winning agency via her LinkedIn contacts and explained how her firm could help with the project as a subcontractor. This took a two-way connection—the person

---

1. http://www.linkedin.com/in/lesleyshackelfordbateman

who introduced Bateman and the CEO who knew one of Bateman's connections—but the CEO responded positively to the introduction. Bateman's firm submitted as part of their bid and won, which resulted in new business for her agency.

SUMMARY

This particular contract was worth $3,000, and it helped open further business opportunities for Bateman and Design4 Marketing. As a regular course of business, Bateman continues to use LinkedIn to identify possible connections in order to bring in new business.

CASE STUDY

Using LinkedIn for the Greater Good

Though this book is focused on using LinkedIn to develop business, there are some great examples of how people have reached out to their networks in order to benefit others. This is one case study in which various aspects of LinkedIn were utilized and hundreds of people benefited. The strategies used in this particular case study can be mirrored by businesses for similar purposes. This advice is especially pertinent if your own company is looking to host or sponsor an event and shows how the power of LinkedIn can help you achieve your marketing objectives.

BACKGROUND

Kevin L. Nichols[1] was invited to join LinkedIn by a friend in 2005. In the invitation, his friend stated that he was using LinkedIn "to enhance his career and to discover inside connections" he didn't know he had. Nichols signed up, made a profile, and has been utilizing the site ever since.

At the time, Nichols was starting his publishing company, KLN Publishing, LLC, and realized that LinkedIn provided him with the opportunity to communicate directly with executives at publishing

---

1. http://www.linkedin.com/in/klnichols

companies such as Random House and Penguin. He created his own LinkedIn Group and realized that a cross section of executives of various industries were enticed to join, which provided him with a direct connection with thought leaders in his industry. In addition, Nichols had a desire to network with others where he worked.

WHAT HAPPENED

Nichols is currently the moderator of the LinkedIn Downtown San Francisco Networking Group. Using the group, he organizes monthly and quarterly events for professionals in order to network and create business opportunities. Due to the fact that many people in the group were unemployed, he decided to organize an employment symposium that focused on improving résumé writing and interviewing skills. Because the people that needed the symposium were unemployed, skeptics of Nichols' idea said that it would take three or four months to plan and it would cost thousands of dollars.

Using LinkedIn, Nichols organized the event for free in one month. He needed a location that could hold at least a hundred people, so he updated his status indicating the need, and within minutes, one of Nichols' colleagues said she might be able to get space at no charge. Through a networking group, others were introduced to Nichols who offered to donate facility space; provide resource materials, career guidance, and placement information; assist with obtaining panelists; and complete the planning stages. After another status update, Nichols obtained two business contacts that agreed to sponsor food for the event. Finally, Nichols relied on his Fortune 500 recruiting contacts to donate time by being panelists and facilitators.

SUMMARY

Nichols often makes requests to his network for various endeavors in which he is involved and he always gets support. In addition to donations for these functions, he also gets solid recommendations for business engagements. He attributes about 75 percent or more of his annual revenue through relationships he has garnered utilizing LinkedIn. "Although it does not replace the need to attend networking functions," Nichols said, "it's invaluable in preserving and maintaining relationships. Moreover, it is essential in creating new ones."

Glossary

Brand   The unique identity of a product, service, or business. In terms of personal branding, this is what differentiates you from everyone else. It highlights your specific skills and experiences and, therefore, marks you as having these particular attributes.

Business-to-business (B2B)   Commerce transactions between two professional entities, such as between a manufacturer and a wholesaler or a wholesaler and a retailer. An example of a B2B transaction would be the sale of leather, laces, and rubber from a wholesaler to a shoemaker.

Business-to-consumer (B2C)   Commerce transactions that take place whereby the end result is the consumer purchasing a service or product. An example of a B2C transaction would be the sale of a completed pair of shoes from a retailer to a consumer.

Cost per click (CPC)   is the amount of money that is paid by an advertiser to a search engine or other Internet platform for a single click on an online advertisement.

Click-through rate (CTR)   The average number of times an ad is clicked per one-hundred impressions. This number is expressed as a percentage. It only measures those people who arrived at a destination site directly through the ad, not those who arrived at the site later on their own accord as a result of seeing the ad.

Closed network   People with whom you personally know or have done business. When you participate in closed networking, you only allow access to those whom you've approved or authenticated.

Content management system (CMS) A collection of procedures or a platform where numerous people can create and manage workflow in a collaborative manner. Many websites are now being built using popular CMS software such as WordPress, Drupal, or Joomla!.

Customer relationship management (CRM) A strategy implemented by a company to manage interactions with customers, clients, and sales prospects. It often involves using technology to organize, automate, and synchronize business processes. The ultimate goal of CRM is to find and attract new clients, nurture and retain current clients, and entice former clients back. Popular CRM platforms include Salesforce, Infusionsoft, InsideView and Microsoft Dynamics.

Facebook (http://www.facebook.com) A social networking site that allows users to include status updates, upload photos, and engage in other features, primarily for personal purposes. Currently recognized as the largest social media website, with more than 500 million active members.[64]

Google juice A term referring to the value that Google gives your website. This value is determined by a number of factors, including having valued and well-regarded websites link to your website and frequently publishing unique, high-quality, relevant, and SEO-friendly content.

Inbound marketing This popular social media marketing doctrine is a strategy focused on being found by potential customers. The founders of Hubspot created the term, and a book of the same name is available.

Long tail In keyword research, an expansion of core, generic, high-volume keyword phrases, which include numerous combinations and permutations of the keywords and their associated or relevant phrases. This term was made popular by a book of the same name written by Chris Anderson.[65]

Pay-per-click (PPC) A type of Internet advertising that directs traffic to websites in which advertisers pay the hosting service when an ad is clicked. These ads are typically tied to keyword phrases relevant to an advertiser's target market when they appear on search engines.

---

64. http://www.facebook.com/press/info.php?statistics
65. http://wind.mn/longtaildef

Referral engine   A chain of reactions that occurs when current customers begin referring your business to others. The ultimate goal with a referral engine is that your business will market itself through its customer base.

Return on investment (ROI)   A measure of performance that evaluates the efficiency of an investment or compares a number of investments.

Search engine marketing (SEM)   A form of Internet marketing that promotes websites by increasing their visibility in search engine results. This is usually done through the use of paid placement, contextual advertising, and paid inclusion.

Search engine optimization (SEO)   The process of improving a website's visibility in search engine results through organic means, such as using specific verbiage on your website and having other websites link back to your site using certain words.

Social media optimization (SMO)   Strategies for using social media activities to attract unique visitors to specific website content. Whereas SEO is focused on driving traffic through search engines, SMO is focused on driving traffic from sources other than search engines.

Spam   Unsolicited bulk electronic messages that receivers consider obtrusive junk. Most people simply disregard or fear malicious intent from spam, so it is prudent to avoid over-sending frequent and irrelevant messages that may potentially be perceived as such.

Twitter (http://www.twitter.com)   A micro-blogging social networking tool that allows users to interact in 140-character messages. Twitter currently boasts more than 200 million users.[66]

Windmill Networking (http://windmillnetworking.com)   Creating a strategic, virtual network utilizing social media and leveraging these relationships for specific personal and professional objectives in the real world as mutual needs arise. A concept created by Neal Schaffer, which is also his brand name.

---

66. http://wind.mn/twitter200

The Production Team

NEAL SCHAFFER, AUTHOR

NEAL SCHAFFER is a consultant, writer, speaker, and recognized leader in helping businesses and professionals leverage the maximum potential of social media. Passionate about helping others through blogging and public speaking, Neal is also a proud member of the Social Media Club and serves on the marketing committee for the United Way of Orange County. Follow Neal on Twitter @NealSchaffer, invite him to connect on LinkedIn at http://www.linkedin.com/in/nealschaffer, buy his stock on Empire Avenue at http://wind.mn/eavinvite, and visit his blog at http://windmillnetworking.com.

JOANNA HAUGEN, LEAD EDITOR

JOANNA HAUGEN is a widely published writer, editor, and blogger for a variety of industries. She is the Las Vegas travel guide writer for BootsnAll; the managing editor for Journey Beyond Travel, an online guide about travel to Morocco; and the community news editor for WorldView, the publication of the National Peace Corps Association. JoAnna also writes the popular travel blog Kaleidoscopic Wandering. Her portfolio can be found at http://www.joannahaugen.com. Connect with JoAnna at http://www.linkedin.com/in/joannahaugen and follow her on Twitter @joanna_haugen.

LOUISE JULIG, COPYEDITOR

LOUISE JULIG is a writer with dozens of article credits in Southern California regional publications since 2005 including *AAA Westways, Carlsbad Magazine, Encinitas Magazine,* and *San Diego Family Magazine.* She also writes the popular blog Thoughts Happen. As a copyeditor she previously edited *Smooth Jazz News* for five years and was co-editor of "Fresh from Elizabeth's Kitchen: Gluten-Free & Allergy-Free Recipes for Healthy, Delicious Meals." Her portfolio can be found at http://www.louisejulig.com. Connect with Louise at http://www.linkedin.com/in/louisejulig and follow her on Twitter @ ThoughtsHappen.

TANYA MAIBORODA, BOOK DESIGNER

TANYA MAIBORODA is a graphic designer and illustrator specializing in books. She has designed many books for clients such as Penguin Group (USA), McGraw-Hill, and Barnes & Noble Books. Her most recent illustrated book is *Read It Yourself Snow White and the Seven Dwarfs* for Ladybird Books in the U.K. She has also been a featured artist at the Hive Gallery in Los Angeles. Her portfolio can be found at http://www.tanyamaiboroda.com. Connect with Tanya at http://www.linkedin.com/in/tanyamaiboroda.

About the Author

NEAL SCHAFFER is recognized as a leader in helping businesses and professionals embrace and strategically leverage the potential of social media. An author, speaker, and social media strategy consultant, Neal has appeared in the Wall Street Journal, Bloomberg Business Week, Yahoo!, and the American Express Open Forum. A graduate of Amherst College, he is also fluent in Mandarin Chinese and Japanese and currently resides in Irvine, California, where he proudly serves on the marketing committee for the United Way of Orange County.

Neal's first book, *Windmill Networking: Understanding, Leveraging & Maximizing LinkedIn,* was a recipient of multiple industry awards and continues to be one of the best-selling books in its genre. In 2011, Neal published this second book, *Maximizing LinkedIn for Sales and Social Media Marketing.* He is currently working on his third book, tentatively titled *Windmill Networking: Maximizing Twitter,* which is expected to be published in late 2011.

As President of Windmills Marketing, a social media strategy consulting practice, Neal has led social media strategy creation, educational workshops, and implementation coaching for a range of B2B and B2C companies including a Fortune 50 software company, a multi-billion dollar nutritional supplements enterprise, and a popular Mexican-American musician. Services provided by Windmills Marketing include:

* Social media strategy consulting
* Social media implementation and strategy coaching
* Custom social media workshops

Neal is also a frequent social media conference speaker and is passionate about educating his audience with content that is custom created to help them truly understand, leverage, and maximize social media for a variety of objectives. Through his speaking engagements, he helps companies and professional associations reach the next level in understanding and strategically implementing social media with compelling content and concrete takeaways.

Neal has spoken in front of thousands of professionals at nearly 100 national and international events including:

- Annual corporate sales events and workshops
- National social media and marketing events such as the Online Marketing Summit, Gravity Summit, LavaCon 2.0, and Gov2.5
- Business events sponsored by CBS Radio and Hartford and Rochester Business Journal
- Corporate webinars sponsored by PR software company Vocus and social CRM startup Nimble
- Professional associations such as the Healthcare Businesswomen's Association (HBA), Public Relations Society of America (PRSA), International Association of Business Communicators (IABC), Young Presidents' Organization (YPO), CEO Trust, Social Media Club, and National Association of Hispanic Real Estate Professionals (NAHREP)

For publishing, consulting, or speaking inquiries, please contact Neal directly through any of the channels below:

EMAIL: neal@windmillnetworking.com
PHONE: (888) 541-3429
WEB: http://windmillnetworking.com
LINKEDIN: http://www.linkedin.com/in/nealschaffer
TWITTER: http://twitter.com/nealschaffer
FACEBOOK: http://www.facebook.com/WindmillNetworking

CPSIA information can be obtained
at www.ICGtesting.com
Printed in the USA
LVOW04s1743120516
487961LV00023B/831/P